Introduction

I have always enjoyed telling stories. As a teacher, I use this practice a great deal—and for various purposes. When I first started in the profession, it provided a way to connect with colleagues and impart a sense of belonging within the teaching community. Oh, the many stories I have compiled after years of doing this! During one particularly memorable school assembly, Jimmy A. shouted, "F#ck the police! No cell can hold me!" as he sprinted from his seat before swooping in and driving off in the solar panel car that was proudly on display. Recounting this story has formed a special bond amongst the staff in attendance that day. Then, there was the time that Marisa was caught red-handed smoking in the student toilets by a staff member and simply replied nonchalantly, "My doctor prescribed it." Such a calm, cool, and collected response would make even the most seasoned staff member pause momentarily to question the validity of Marisa's excuse, then ponder how much society has changed since they started in the profession way back when.

Over time, I have honed my ability to use these and other stories to paint a picture of what teaching *really* involves to outsiders. Not only do my stories help me walk non-teaching folk through the ins and out of the daily events and long-term lessons and rewards of teaching, but they act as a behind-the-scenes look at the profession. I have learned the value in finding just the right story to share with the many bozos with whom I have crossed paths who say things like, "You get twelve weeks holiday a year. How hard can it be!?" It always brings a smile to my face when they finally realize the truth. It's a beautiful thing to witness their smug demeanour fade into stark disbelief and embarrassment as they realise just how much is involved in teaching—and playing such a significant role in the lives of young people. I guess, finally, telling these stories may just be my way of processing the day-to-day intricacies of teaching: a way to unwind and make sense of it all. Or, quite frankly, maybe I just need to focus on finding a way to laugh out of fear that otherwise, I will lose myself to insanity.

I had always told myself that at one point, I would start to write these stories down, never really knowing if I would actually do so. Then, when COVID-19 began, a strange thing happened... Free time became a thing! I seized the opportunity, and I got busy. During this writing period, I had just qualified for my first round of long-service leave. It truly felt like just the other day that I was a fresh-faced graduate heading up to the country to teach. Somehow, I had blinked my eyes, and ten years had flown by. The writing process afforded the wonderful benefit of reliving the many memories I share within the following pages: the characters I have met along the way and the experiences I have had (both good and bad). One thing is for sure: the teaching profession's breadth, depth, and overall complexity never ceases to amaze me.

Let me tell you a little more about me. I am thirty-five years old at the time of writing. I started teaching at twenty-three years old in rural Western Australia, and although I felt like I was mature enough to handle it at the time, in reality, most days, I would constantly remind myself to 'fake it till you make it.' I thought if I acted confident enough, the students would have no choice but to believe what I said... and that I knew what I was doing. I have always taught high school mathematics in tough schools throughout my teaching career. I did have a stint at a senior campus, and when I tell stories to colleagues, they consider it the gold standard within the profession. Nevertheless, the school did present its own set of difficulties.

Who is this book for? First, it's for anyone considering or about to start teaching. I applaud you! I hope you can learn a thing or two from my trials and tribulations. Second, it's for anyone who has already been teaching for a while. If this is the case, I have one thing to say: You are a star! Sometimes we just need to sit back, have a good laugh, and remind ourselves that these crazy things really *did* (and continue to) happen! Finally, it's for anyone outside of the teaching realm who wonders what actually goes on in the day-to-day life of a teacher. Let me tell you, though, these stories are only the tip of the iceberg. They have nowhere near done the profession justice.

Finally, these stories have been kept short on purpose, as I am always conscious of people's time. I just wanted it to be something you could pick up and quickly find a passage that may help you through your day. Maybe you had a horrific day, and you need some relief. Pick up this book, and let me guide you through some of my worst days. Maybe you are sitting at home watching your latest TV series, and suddenly you are reminded that you have year nine Dream Team first thing tomorrow. Pick up the book and read about the time I was locked in my room (while teaching) and had to wait an hour for the rescue team to arrive. Maybe within these pages you will find even the smallest amount of help to make your life easier heading forward. If so, I hope you will share with me as it will surely bring a smile to my face. After all, we are in one of the most challenging professions in the world, so let's make sure we look after one another! These just happened to be the first fifty stories that came to me.

My Doctor prescribed me cigarettes

My First-Ever Lesson

I started teaching at twenty-three, and it was a lot of responsibility at the time, especially as I still had the face of a 16-year-old. I will never forget my first day in class. I was sitting at my teacher's desk feeling all mature and adult-like when my students entered and just started going to town on me, yelling to each other, "Oi, who's the new kid?" and, "Hey, new kid, that's the teacher's desk; you're back here with the rest of us!" It took me half the lesson to convince them that I was actually their teacher. They just kept shouting out, "Ooooooooo! I can't wait till the teacher gets here and puts this new kid in his place."

The lesson went from bad to worse. Every time I opened my mouth, they timed it perfectly and spoke over me, shouting most of the time. I would think back to what I had learned at University. Give them wait time and be patient. I thought to myself, if I stick to this pace, we would still be covering Term One concepts deep into Term Four.

Twenty minutes from the end of the lesson, the topic's excitement became too much for a group of lads at the back. At first, I saw a few fingers pointed towards each other, then punches landed. A chair was thrown for good measure. I managed to make my way from the front of the class and got in between it all, hoping to slow down the energy. A few students were sent outside, a few more to the head of the department, and one to the Deputy's office. I remember thinking to myself... all this from a lesson on percentages. I never knew multiples of ten percent would get the blood boiling that much.

The end of the lesson came, and I managed to re-centre myself. Little did I know the high point of my day was still yet to come. The Mathematics Department's office was down towards the back of the school, and it had large floor-to-ceiling glass doors which you pull to enter. Outside, there were a few picnic tables scattered around where students would sit during breaks. I must have still been a little shaken, and I was rushing down to the office. I misjudged the situation and flew headfirst into the doors. I took a minute to compose myself, reassuring myself that no one saw. I looked around; everyone had seen. Someone then yelled out, "The cleaners have levelled up with their Windex game this year, Sir, haven't they?" It took me nearly nine months to get rid of the nickname Windex.

Best of the Best (The Hardest Class I Ever Taught)

I have always taught in hard-to-staff, low socio-economic schools. Classes can get a little rough at times, but if you stick it out, the bond you can build with these students is incredible. In saying that, I met my match about three to four years ago. I have since switched schools, but I will always look back on this class and say, "Gee whiz, there were some characters!"

That particular year, I was assigned the bottom Year Seven group. Before the year even began, I had to conduct numerous planning sessions with the previous primary-grade teachers of these students to help predict what to expect. It felt like I was in one of those scenes in the movies when they are putting a crew together to do a bank job. You know, like this guy is good at this certain skill, so he gets in the crew, she has this talent, so she gets chosen as well. Instead, the primary teachers would point to a group of names on my student roll and simply announce, "See these students here? They have these blends of learning disorders, and see these students over here? They have these assortments of behavioural disorders." "This particular student here hasn't lasted longer than fifteen minutes inside a classroom in his schooling career."

There were only fifteen students in the class, but they truly were the best of the best. I used to have to line these guys up at the start of the lesson, and it was like trying to round up stray kittens. Lessons were sixty minutes, but any more than four to five minutes on a task and their attention span fell apart. If they couldn't do something straight away, they would lose their minds and start verbally abusing each other. If it got to the point where I had to send a student outside for continually misbehaving, I had to put the room on lockdown as they would try to get back into class and prison break the others. One of my students had a hard time processing his anger. At one point in his journey in education, he had been given a long, padded paddle as an anger management tool. The deal was, anytime he felt his anger rising, he would take himself out and start smashing the large metal gate outside our room, and this would calm him back down. I had another student who was gifted with the pen until he had to use it for any type of schoolwork. Anytime he was outside, he would sneak off to different classrooms and discover new and exciting ways to position his pen in the door to lock students in their rooms. Teachers would phone me mid-lesson, pleading with me to come and set them free. To top it all off, there was a special needs room twenty to thirty metres across the pathway from our room. A tall girl in there would occasionally escape, making her way down to our class to join in the fun. She was always super-excited when she arrived and started banging on the windows and yelling. The kids loved her. They saw her coming then shouted, 'Here she comes, sir,' then seconds later, they joined her outside, heading off to storm the aisles trying to incite a student uprising. I had a pre-service teacher with me at one point during this time. She was ready to change the world on day one. On day two, she came in to observe this class and never made it back to finish the prac.

A Boy Named Danger

I had taken up the position of Year Eight coordinator when I first met Danger. People told me I was young to take on the role and that it would be a great career advancement opportunity. To be honest, I was having a hard enough time trying to organise four teachers to supervise a lunchtime detention roster, so it felt like serious career advancement was far from my doorstep.

In these pastoral care positions, you are seen as the caretaker for your designated year group—the link between students, teachers, and administration, as it was described to me. Basically, I was just a person to take some of the load off the Deputy. An upside was that I did get to work with students beyond my immediate classes, and boy, did I meet some characters.

Danger first crossed my path when he was referred to me by several of his teachers for playing up in class. He would head down to the Mathematics Office where I was stationed, and we began our process. I had no real disciplinary powers, and he gleaned never-ending satisfaction from continually missing class. We would talk. He was open, and I must admit he had the wool pulled over my eyes at first. He was a little guy. His backpack was half his size (it was a big pack, but still), and he was always smiling. I thought at first maybe that this was just one big misunderstanding, but his true character soon revealed itself.

Danger had a special gift—being able to completely demolish school rubbish bins in a matter of seconds when his rage took hold. These were not the small bins either. His preference was the big wheelie bins, which stood around the campus. He was methodical in his process. He started with flying kicks to knock the bins over, then merged into a series of jumping attacks to finish them off. I think I may have been present when he first developed his 'seek and destroy' senses. I had been called out of class to deal with him. By the time I got there, he was already in full rampage mode. I remember he stopped and looked at me briefly when I first arrived. However, within seconds he spotted the bin behind me, and then, it was on. Complete fury and destruction. Over the next several months, his bond with the 'wheelies' became even stronger, his process in anger management. As time went on, I was able to fine-tune my approach. I knew by the time he had reached the bins, the rage wave would be coming to an end within a few minutes as he would be exhausted, and then we would be able to talk. Not about maths homework, though, because this would send him into another round fit of rage, a lesson I learned the hard way.

The crowning event occurred when I was on duty one day. Danger had swept into my area a few minutes earlier. He seemed calm, although that could change in a moment. A few minutes later, he erupted. A performance for the ages. I was about fifty metres or so from him when there was an altercation between him and another student. By the time I started moving towards them, Danger had already been triggered, and it was on. There was a line of bins evenly spaced around the yard. Danger made light work of this. He went on his rampage, obliterating every bin as he walked toward me. As he entered my space, I said nothing and raised a finger, pointing in the direction of the Deputy's office. Without saying a word, he continued his path of destruction all the way to the office. As I followed him, I couldn't help but admit I was a little impressed by his commitment to the task.

This is the day I began to refer to him as Danger because wherever he was, Danger was not far behind.

The Extractor

"The pen is mightier than the sword!" a student once announced to me moments before launching his pen at me.

Having to extract students from colleagues' classes can be a tricky business. Each student is different, and every student has a tonne of things happening to them daily. Usually, teachers only know the surface issues. Just before walking into a class for an 'extraction,' I prepare myself for the unknown and remind myself that no two days in teaching are ever alike.

At one school, I became quite well known for heading into classes at teachers' request and removing students who had been misbehaving. In one particular Year Seven class, there was a fella who was not overly enthusiastic about learning. He was, however, incredibly enthusiastic about causing mayhem. I remember the first time I walked into his class after he had been giving his teacher a hard time. He was running up and down the aisles, causing all kinds of mischief. I assumed a posture of authority, extending my 6-foot-4 frame to look as tall as possible while calmly motioning for him to head over to me. For most students at this young age, they are still terrified of authority figures; it usually takes till year nine until they turn into complete anarchists. This guy relished being in the spotlight, launching his pen into me from a few meters away. I entered hostage negotiation mode and calmly mentioned that if he ever wanted to see lunchtime again, he would follow me. The extraction was successful. Over the following few months, he and I became well acquainted. He would play up in class, and I would take on the elements to remove him. Then he would come down and sit with me in the office to complete work.

There is another side to this as well, however, when students are unfairly treated by teachers. I was involved with a particular year ten class at one time. The teacher was not the most understanding, with most situations going straight to a power struggle. The classroom environment was tragic. I tried working with the teacher during the class, but not a whole heap ended up getting through. After a short while of removing students from the class, I became known to the students as 'security.' Every time I entered the room, they started throwing out excuses as to why they didn't have their photo ID with them, but I was still to let them in the club. I was fond of the class and made it a point to interact with the students a little when heading in. By the end of the year, the students would see me coming, knowing that I was there to remove a student, so they would all break out in a perfect chorus of, "Hey, hey, hey, goodbye!"

I was lucky to have good mentors earlier on in my career. At one of my first schools, I was teaching at a hard-to-staff school with a seasoned head of department. He would slip into classes and elegantly remove students from classes unnoticed and at ease. Like any seasoned veteran, he had his go-to moves. On days he had to remove multiple students from different classes, he grouped them all up and formed 'the positive influence line.' He took the group of students around his department, where he had positioned positive behaviour posters for their viewing pleasure. My favourite one, though, was if he started to receive the usual suspects, he took his intervention to the next level, having students count out the individual bricks on patches of school space. As they counted, he reminded students that there were easier ways to progress in learning Mathematics and that maybe they needed to reconsider their behaviour in class.

Maths Camp

Maths Camp is exactly what it sounds like—a camp based around maths activities—and before you jump off your seats with excitement, there was a bonus. The camp dates also fell on the weekend of the biggest festival in town (I was still in the country at this time)! You can imagine just how excited the students were to give up their usual 'fun times' to pick up the pen and Sudoku set instead. But we found a way to make it work.

As we were located pretty far north in the state and the camp was to be held a few hours drive south from the city, we would have to fly down. From memory, there were twelve students all up. I had nine with me. The other three students would be accompanied down by another teacher and meet us at the camp on the second day. I knew I was off to a good start when a few of the students played around on the flight down—minimal disturbance, but still. The flight steward started to tell all of them off, including me. I had to stop her halfway through and confess that I was their teacher even though I had the face of a sixteen-year-old.

When the aeroplane landed, we were loaded onto the bus. This part of the ride was seamless, and I briefly reassured myself that the worst was behind us. We arrived at the camp and were pointed in the direction of our dorms. I dropped the girls off first at their dorm and told them I would be back once I had the boys sorted. By the time I returned to their dorm, a hostile takeover had occurred. The dorms were shared with a few other schools, and there were twenty-five beds in the dorm. My team had turned the place upside down, taking all the best beds, making sure they were all close together. After various 'acts of persuasion,' I managed to have the girls return everything to how it was pre-take over.

The night's activities were to be maths games. I have never had to sell anything so hard in my life, but I think I pulled it off during the walk from the dorms to the games arena. Mind you, I was reminded several times that, "Sir, you told us that this camp was just going to be an escape down to the city, and we would barely have to spend time at the camp." I seemed to have erased that part from memory.

There were a few highlights from the night:

- During a chess game, one of my students ended up in checkmate from a well-put-together chain of moves from her opponent. When the opponent called, "checkmate!" and went to shake hands, my student picked up her opponent's King and stated, "Checkmate this!" as she launched it across the room.
- One student wouldn't participate in anything and told another teacher to get f#cked when she was asked. Nothing beats being a teacher and getting disciplined by another teacher for your students' behaviour.
- My post-games night speech bordered on one of the best uniting addresses of my career. During the walk back to our dorms, I pulled the squad into a private space and stood on one of the nearby benches, professing to my team that now was the time we needed to come together to show these schools what we were made of.

I want to claim that the turnaround in the students' behaviour over the coming days was due to my rousing words. Still, I have a feeling it may have just been the combination of a good night's sleep and the arrival of the spiritual leader (the experienced teacher) the next day. I actually know it was the latter, as pretty much every teacher present for the remainder of camp went out of their way to mention to me how much more well-behaved the students were compared to the first night.

Little Mate and His Anger Pole

I walked into the staffroom this particular morning to find the dreaded pink relief slip sitting in my pigeonhole. Our relief coordinator always told us that he made sure he spread the relief load out evenly, but it did seem that the younger, less difficult teachers (which was me at the time) would stack them up.

The relief I had picked up that day was for a Year Eight English class. Fantastic, I thought to myself. The other day, I told a student there was a silent 'K' at the start of the word neck, so this class would be in for a treat having my expertise for the period. I picked up my belongings and my bottom lip and headed off to the room.

I had not read the lesson left for me till I was about halfway to the room, and not being able to understand four of the first six words, I decided that I would create a lesson on the fly. Here is how it went.

We started with some icebreakers. After the icebreakers, we went into spelling. As outlined above, this is far from a strength of mine, but I decided to adopt a 'fake it till you make it' approach. I sounded out the word to the students, then, after a few minutes, listed the chosen words on the whiteboard behind me. I had to consult Google numerous times for the correct spelling, which did reassure me that I had pursued the right path in teaching Mathematics and not English.

We finally transitioned into a documentary study, which was part of the lesson that had been left for me. The students were still hanging in there, except for a little fella who had taken himself from his desk to the bean bags at the back of the classroom. I kept an eye on him but could see that his mood was starting to change. A few minutes later, he was rocketing towards the door outside. I looked at a few of the other students, and they told me not to worry as this was just my man's process; he just needed to leave for a bit. I watched out from the classroom and could see my man searching in a bush nearby. He seemed to be getting more and more distressed until, finally, he disappeared entirely under the bush only to return with a metal pole in hand. He then wandered over to a rusty metal frame that was sticking out of the ground across the garden and started hammering into it like no tomorrow. When I walked over and asked him what he was doing, he told me he wouldn't be much longer and that this was just his process.

He did return to class later, after stashing his calming aid (metal pole) back under the bush from where it came. For the remaining twenty-five minutes of the class, he worked quietly by himself and managed to finish the majority of his work.

On the walk back to the office, I did think to myself, have I been going about behaviour management all wrong so far in my time teaching? When I made it back to the pigeonholes and saw another pink relief slip waiting for me, I quickly turned around and went on the hunt for my man's calming aid.

The Weapon of Choice

I still have the look of the young teacher's face imprinted in my mind as she came storming towards the office from her class one day. She took a moment to compose herself before asking me if I could head into her Year Nine 'dream team' class and remove a dildo that had made an appearance and that the students were now attacking each other with.

It is always interesting to head into these situations. You never quite know how to prepare yourself. Usually, as I walk to the class, I try to have several scenarios run through my mind with alternative game plans for each one. This sounds great in theory, but very rarely do they line up with the reality of the situation. This day was no different.

Entering the class, I could sense the energy in the room. Although most students were now back in their chairs, they were far from completing their problems on congruent triangles, which I could see neatly displayed on the teacher's whiteboard at the back of the room. I could see the weapon of choice now displayed proudly, front and centre, on the teacher's desk, with a note attached to it stating, "Use me, I am bored." There was a moment of silence before a student seized his opportunity and spoke up. "Are you here for your weekend tool, Sir?" The room erupted in laughter. I did my best to bite down hard on mine. After a quick round of verbal sparring, I removed the two ringleaders and their weapon of choice, walking them each to separate buddy room classes, keeping the weapon close by but out of sight as I moved quickly toward the office.

Our fearless leader (head of the department) happened to be away that day, so I was a little perplexed with the process of appropriately handling a dildo during school hours. After consultation with my other colleagues in the office at the time, we decided it was best that we lay the weapon to rest in a drawer, and I would explain the situation to our department head the next day. We all recognized that trying to do so in words at the time would be doing a great injustice to the entire situation. The option coming in at a close second was to strap the dildo to our boss's chair and hope he would notice it before sitting down.

The Gatekeeper

I have never been so on edge around a simple lock and classroom door before.

At one time, I used a demountable classroom, with a veranda between it and the other end. Outside of these two rooms, there was nothing but green grass separating us from the rest of the school. Usually, there was only one class at a time scheduled out there; however, one year, we hit the jackpot. I was teaching Year Nine 'F Troop,' while my colleague taught Year Eights—with both classes running simultaneously.

Our approaches to behaviour management were a little different. I was more militant with organisation and pushing students to be on time to class and get the work done. My colleague was more free-spirited and believed in an organic approach to teaching, where learning was more of an option and staying in class was not high on the agenda. Not saying that one method is more effective than the other, but there were times we had difficulties.

This was when I first crossed paths with the student who became known to me as 'The Gatekeeper.' This student had a gift, and it certainly wasn't his in-depth understanding of Trigonometry. He had the ability to lock a class in their rooms with any object he could find nearby. He was a quiet little lad who wouldn't say much and kept to himself, according to my colleague. He established his routine early on. A few minutes towards the end of a lesson, he would drift quietly outside and jam something, usually a writing tool, between the lock and the door, keeping the rest of his class locked inside. Initially, I didn't know what was happening and thought it was rather strange that year eight students wanted to stay behind and continue studying into their break time. It soon dawned on me that they had no other choice. As time went on and I became more involved in the rescue missions, I developed a plan of attack. I would leave the door to my classroom-wide open and make sure to position myself in the doorway towards the end of the period. I was able to see directly into my colleague's class, and if the student was about to make a move for the door, I would foil the attack. Eventually, the lock-ins came to an end.

As time went on, this student's attendance started to wavier. He would miss months of school at a time. It was a shame. I thought we had bonded over his attempts at mass lock-ins and my counter-surveillance efforts at keeping the area safe. Shucks, he had even shot me a smile one day when I caught him moments before his attempt. The memory that stands out most occurred when I was teaching and had not seen The Gatekeeper for a good couple of months, so I had become lazy and complacent in my awareness of the door. I remember hearing a slight sound around my classroom door mid-lesson but hadn't thought much about it. At the end of the lesson, I tried to open the door to release my class with no luck. I tried a few more times then saw a figure appear on the grass outside, waving at us with a giant grin across his face before he took off. Now, these were the times before I carried my phone with me to class, and unlike my colleague's classroom, mine had been built in the 1970s, so the windows would barely open, certainly not enough for a teacher or student to be able to escape. Eventually, we got word out and were released. The best part of the story was that the student had not even attended any classes that day but instead had just decided to get dressed up in his school uniform and lock a few people in a room.

From that day forward, for the remainder of my days out in this room, every time I heard the slightest noise around my door, I would spring to action, rushing outside to make sure no mishappenings were about to occur.

Inspiring the Masses

Robin Williams in *Dead Poets Society*, Michelle Pfeiffer in *Dangerous Minds*, and Samuel Jackson in *Coach Carter* were my early career mentors. When they spoke, their students listened.

Public speaking is a fear for most people. When I finally decided that I would become a teacher, I had pangs of panic run through me, knowing that I would have to get up and speak in front of people. I would always second-guess myself, trying to remind myself to remain confident and in control while '*Back Seat Johnny*' was yelling out at the top of his lungs, "Sir, you need to raise that pre-pubescent voice of yours; it barely reaches the back row!"

During my days participating in team sports, I was the unfortunate victim of my fair share of 'sprays' from various coaches. For anyone who is not familiar with the term, it is equivalent to verbally laying out a player, hoping that they will rise stronger from the onslaught and take on the accountability needed to improve their performance in the future. Now, in the classroom, I am not going to this extreme, but it made me think how a few chosen words here and there can help bolster student motivation.

You can't just walk into a room and start tearing students apart, nor should you. It is highly unprofessional, and you are likely to cause more harm than good. There must be a message. I have observed patterns of behaviour in classes where I have students with behavioural issues. These students tend to feel overwhelmed faster, are quick to anger, and have a deep fear of failure. At other times, they may have consumed a one-litre energy drink just before stepping into your class, so no amount of targeted words will help. Good luck. If I am in a cycle of a few lessons where students are starting to act up, I will stop the class and launch into some chosen words around accountability and perseverance. At other times I will talk about the power of self-control and resilience in hard times. If you can strike the right balance between long-term rewards and overcoming adversity in your message, beautiful things can start to happen.

Timing is everything. There are only a finite number of times you can stop the class and launch into some chosen words in the attempt to motivate before you reach the point of diminishing returns. I have experienced this firsthand. In classes where the going has been challenging from the start, this method has worked well initially. Students are taken by surprise and genuinely reflect on what has been said. When I have started to overuse this technique, students will still stop and listen out of respect before returning to the chokehold that they had been applying to a peer earlier.

Authenticity is crucial. You must develop your own words based on your unique classroom environment. I made a breakthrough with a class one time. They were a hardened bunch of Year Nines that were starting to spiral as a class, so I stopped them at one point during a lesson and launched into some rousing words of wisdom. Now, it just happened that I had watched the movie *Coach Carter* with Samuel Jackson a few nights prior, so my speech was completely plagiarized, but it had worked. The only problem now was that I couldn't go back. I spent most of my nights for a solid week after school on YouTube searching for motivational speeches, making sure that it would be an obscure enough reference that the students would not have come across it. This continued to work for a little while longer until, eventually, I used a reference which most of them had heard before. I knew the gig was up when they started quoting the words to me even before I had opened my mouth.

Not Just My Teaching Persona

My mother was a teacher for many years. When I was young, I would ask her why she would not take up a position at our local school—the one that I happened to be attending. I thought it was just that she didn't want to deal with me and my gremlin ways in class and then cook and clean at night for me too. This turned out to be partially true. She affirmed it to me one day, then explained that she also did not want to see her students around the local neighbourhood outside of class time. Personal time was necessary.

I remember when I first started going out for nights on the town and would, on rare occasions, cross paths with an ex-teacher of mine. Usually, this happened later in the evening at a bar somewhere, so the barriers between past students and teachers had come tumbling down. This was further evident in our conversations. Ranging anywhere from inquiries into my personal life and progression to statements such as, "I damn right hated you while you were in my class," with one teacher even admitting that on more than one occasion, he would bang his head against the wall when he saw me heading towards his lesson. I guess I just found these interactions odd. When you spend so many years viewing these people as teachers, you almost forget they have other sides to them.

In saying that, here are some of the encounters I have experienced when seeing my own students outside of school:

I was out on a date one night many years ago when I came across some ex-students who had recently graduated from university and were out celebrating. The date had been going fine; there had been minimal talk about previous experiences with algebra, so we were off and running and, at one point, had ended up at a bar in the city. Halfway through a conversation in a crowded area, my ex-students came swanning across, ending up in between us.

"Sir, I can't believe you are here. Is this your wife?"

The next student took up the lead and chimed in, "Sir, we didn't know you were married; why didn't you tell us?"

When the last comment came out, "Sir, shouldn't you two be at home looking after your children? This is very irresponsible parenting!" I knew I could no longer let the student act go on as I glanced over and saw my date's eyes starting to swim across her face, not realising the students were just winding us up. I made the introductions, much to my ex-students' delight at seeing me squirm having to introduce my date.

"Shouldn't you guys be at home sharing a Sudoku or something mathematically romantic like that?" We both burst out laughing, and for the remainder of the conversation, they were on their best behaviour.

Coming across students at their place of work is always amusing for me. Working in a country town, I regularly crossed paths with students at the local grocery store, being it was the only one in town. Usually, they would be working on the checkout. "Good to see all that math education is taking you to the lofty heights at this place," I would exclaim as I arrived at the checkout, thinking my wit had hit an all-time high.

"You were my teacher last year, Sir; I wouldn't be trying to pass the buck on this one," is one of the better replies I received. Being young at the time, and with my motivation for cooking peaking at zero percent, fast food became a regular thing. However, there were those nights where I would walk into the restaurant only to turn and head straight back out again after noticing a student I had a run-in with earlier in the day during class now working the grill—and responsible for handling my food. You can never be entirely sure of the right ingredients of the special sauce, and I wasn't going to leave it up to wishful thinking. Forced overnight fasting became a 'thing' for me at one point.

Over the years, the once white-hot rage I experienced while driving in traffic has started to mellow. There are still times when something will happen, and I will feel anger rush through me. These days I can settle back down quickly. This was not always the case. Driving to and from school, I become super vigilant within the zone of ten to fifteen kilometres from the school. That is when I start to notice student drivers nearby, as most students live locally. However, this is not always true. I was on the main road one day, having finished school for the day, and already a good twenty to thirty minutes into my trip. Not happy with the ability of the driver next to me to merge into traffic, I offered them a little advice with a particular choice of words, none of which were flattering. I made sure to add nonverbal cues to further punctuate my feelings, all through an open window, with the flow of traffic moving at about thirty km per hour. When the driver's face was finally revealed to me, I felt a wave of nausea rise through me, realising it was a student I was currently teaching. To make the experience that much better, the student was still on her learner's permit, and I had not identified the plates clearly displayed on each windscreen. I had to lean over and start apologising profusely to both the student and her father, who was sitting in the passenger's seat.

I heard the father ask, "Dear, who is this?"

The daughter replied simply, "It's Okay, Dad. It is just my Maths teacher."

Life in the Wrong Lane

"He will attend every class, and he will keep his mouth shut unless he is required to talk." I was halfway through a lesson on interpreting graphs with my year ten students when the deputy principal saddled up beside me, a new student quietly standing next to him. I had just spent the previous twenty minutes working with a small group of students, explaining the difference between the horizontal and vertical axis of a graph. Being that this had lasted nineteen minutes longer than I had anticipated, the interruption was welcomed. I introduced myself quickly to the student and gave him a brief rundown of the lesson, then watched him make his way to the back of the class, where he sat in silence till the bell went.

I made my way to the staffroom after the lesson. I needed caffeine and a walk to help clear my mind. When I arrived, I overheard a few colleagues talking in the corner about this new student. They were all agreeing that he was no good as he had already made his way through three schools in that year alone. "He is bad news, and I can't wait for him to make his way out of here. It will only be a quick stay," one of the more seasoned teachers stated.

For the first week or two, the student didn't say much in class. He was a little fella from the wrong side of the tracks. Reading through his file, I found it filled with the usual awful things. Abuse, parental (hard) drug use, abandonment. I felt like running this file around to all the teachers who had already cast judgement on him. I wanted to shout from the top of my lungs, "Maybe let's give this kid a chance and a little support and see what comes from it." But I knew it would fall on deaf ears. Instead, I intended to focus my efforts on providing a classroom environment that could help him grow. Sure, if he picked up a number fact here or there, this would be handy as well. As the weeks rolled on, he opened up more, and I started to see another side to him. He still wasn't sitting down completing a whole lot of work, but he was respectful most of the time, which was a heap more than he was achieving in other classes.

There are a few memories from this time that I now look back on and laugh at. The first was, he had an entourage follow him around the school. The main objective of his crew was to shield him from other students (the fans) as he had become quite the little socialite in just a small span of time. The other major task for one of the crew members was to carry his bag. It wasn't unusual to see him walking in the centre of the group around the school with one of his members at the front with four different bags strapped to him. As time went on, his character grew. He would usually greet me at my door as he arrived for maths class, emerging from the middle of his posse to remind me that, "The mother f$$$ing King of Math is here, and I'm about to f##k all this number s##t up."

Another time, our block of classrooms had been broken into over the weekend, including my room. He ushered me off to the side during a lesson the following week and asked, "Sir, if I were to know where the projector was, would anyone get in trouble if it was returned?" He let me think about it for a minute or two. The next thing I knew, he had scaled the fence next to our classroom and was walking around in the nearby bushland. He returned five minutes later with the projector!

Throughout the year, he had been making progress in class. A little support and someone to believe in him had given him a needed boost. Unfortunately, his performance outside of the classroom did not match his performance inside, as he continued to get in trouble with the law. He was taken one morning on a bus with other juvenile offenders and a few police officers to a nearby juvenile detention centre as an educational strategy by the police in the area at the time. The idea was to show at-risk boys where they could end up if they kept playing up. I remember the bus arriving back at school, pulling up a few hundred metres from my room. He came bundling in. I put the lesson on hold as he took centre stage and told us all about his adventure that day. We all started to lose our minds when he told us that at the very end of the excursion, he was given an ultimatum by the police. The choices were either to return on the bus to school or to go get a haircut back on the yard. He told us he took one look at the size of the fellas out there and responded to the police, "There is no way they will touch my rat's tail today."

The student ended up moving on from our school the following year. I have since lost contact with him, but I hope he has managed to find some stability and peace in his life.

Leg Day

Nothing better than being bullied by a group of Year Ten female students as you walk to and from your classroom.

I had just transitioned from a classroom in the main block out to a demountable on the oval. As much as I was enjoying the perks of independence, there were some drawbacks. The room was quite a walk from the office, so I had to make sure my organisation was on point, or I would spend half the lesson running to and from my room. The room was also built in the '80s with minimal upkeep over the years, so it resembled more of a cage than a classroom, which is precisely what students would fondly refer to it as. There were thirty chairs in the room; twenty were broken in some way. Finally, the air conditioner worked only two days during the summer. To know which two days would put you on the same pedestal as some of the greatest oracles of our time.

The year was 2012, but the cage didn't believe in keeping up with the times and still operated with chalk and blackboard. This was handy for me as, at the best of times, my handwriting skills are well below an acceptable standard. With chalk, it got a whole lot worse. During these days, I entered a new realm of unrecognisable characters. "Sir, is that the letter z or number two?" the students would ask. It was neither, but I didn't have the stomach to tell them.

Next to the cage were two slightly more modern demountables. To get back to the Mathematics Office, I had to pass them. The sights I would see. Students would be throwing items at each other, yelling at one another. I even foiled a student's escape one time. His head was hanging halfway out the window with his bag attached. It was impressive he had gotten so far undetected. The look on his face when I told him, "Mate, I have got you. May as well pull yourself back inside and get on with the lesson," was priceless.

Enter the Polynesian trio: three Year Ten girls (all from Polynesia), all of whom I had taught in separate classes the previous year. They were now all in the same Maths class and had become the overlords of the thin passage of territory between my classroom and the office. They were all good girls, cheeky but kind-hearted. They were quick on the uptake as well. They noticed that my recent gym sessions had mostly been targeting my upper body and that I had been neglecting leg workouts. They mentioned to me one day as I was passing that I wasn't spending the time necessary to grow this muscle group. Another day when I was walking past, one of the three wise ladies called out, "Sir, you know you can't skip leg day; it is the most important day of them all!" The other two started to laugh, and I couldn't help but laugh as well.

From then on, I was no longer known to them as Sir, but "Leg Day," and any time I had to make a move to pass their room, it was a bombardment of leg day jokes.

This Lesson Went South Quick

I thought I had reached a point in my career where I had all these types of lessons out of me. I mean the type of lesson where you have everything prepared and know exactly what your students' learning needs are, only to find three minutes into the lesson, it wasn't meant to be.

This used to stress me out. I remember writing my first-ever lesson plan. I had everything planned in intervals of two to three minutes. If I didn't have a piece of instruction go exactly how I had planned, or an activity was slightly off, I could sense it, and I could feel the disappointment build. I would always put up a confident front to the students, but deep down, I felt like I was moments away from panic, and the lesson was spiralling out of control. As the years have rolled on, and I have experienced the most dreaded situations that can and will happen in a classroom environment, I have grown a lot calmer.

I once taught at a senior (mature age) campus. The students ranged anywhere from 16 years of age upwards. One lesson was after lunch, and I had everything prepared and ready to go. In my mind, it was going to be a bamboozler of a lesson, the type where the students would stand and applaud by the end. Instead, the students slowly made their way to class in singles and pairs with nothing more than a mumbled hello and a level of apathy that was anything but inspiring. I knew it was going to be a doozy from the start. There were sixteen students on the class list; however, only six or seven would consistently turn up to class. Tough gig, I know, but trust me, I will get there.

Amongst the regular attendees was a student from China who barely spoke English at the time and had only been in the country for less than a year. Most of our conversation was done through smiles and overemphasised pointing gestures. I had the feeling she just thought I was mad. Student number two was a middle-aged man with a cognitive function impairment. Again, someone with an incredible character, unfortunately, his short-term memory was not the best, and most concepts seemed to become lost once he left the classroom for the day. His time management skills kept me on my toes, sometimes arriving an hour early to class, then at other times fifteen minutes late, with a few arrival times occurring five minutes from the end of the lesson. Suspect number three was a Middle Eastern lady who also had only been in the country for a short time. Her command of English was quite good; her command of numeracy was not so good. Her self-confidence, however, was out of this world. She was the kind of student that would answer every question I would throw to the whole class. She was barely ever correct, but for the short amount of time between when the words would leave her mouth till I processed the answer, in her mind, she was invincible. One day we had a new student arrive at the class as well. More on her in a moment.

Lessons were ninety minutes in length. I would use the first twenty to thirty minutes of the class to focus on a skill set to get the students warmed up and their minds in thinking mode. In this lesson, we were working on number facts. Factors, multiples, all that good stuff. In my mind, when I had planned the lesson the previous night, I had seen a lot of potential. I would be the guiding light to any student who had missed out on or misunderstood these concepts previously. In reality, when it took the students three different attempts to copy the title down correctly, I knew the tremendous educational breakthrough would be on hold for the moment.

We headed into the topic focus for the lesson. After I had worked through several examples as a whole class, I thought we would be off and running, but this wasn't the case. An explanation I had planned to take three to four minutes was nearing ten minutes, even after I had cut it off short when I noticed one student had fallen into a deep sleep mid-explanation. I decided to change tack quickly and had students write down their attempts to solve the problems on their mini (personal) whiteboards and then hold them up to show me. Out of six students, one had the right answer, and only one more was in the ballpark. The remaining answers ranged from numbers that did not make any rational sense to a quick sketch of a male appendage. Not to worry, shake it off, I told myself. Round two went similarly; however, this time, one of the students had written their name as the answer. My confidence was on a steep decline. For the next round, I decided to call on students individually for their answers. It was a three-minute-long period of chaos. The new student started smashing her desk, then ran outside when I asked her first for the answer. My mature age fella asked me if I could re-explain the concept. The only problem was, he had become disorientated and gone back through his notebook and was referring to a concept from three weeks prior. Then, he wanted me to check his homework, something which I had already done twice. Finally, my Middle Eastern lady had written down a plethora of answers. Sadly, after spending a few minutes checking over them, none were remotely correct. We then went to war for a good few minutes discussing in detail the correct answers to each section.

I left the class that day reminded it doesn't matter how much experience you think you have or how many situations you think you have seen. Teaching will always provide you with the lessons that humble you.

Catching Students Truanting

I was in Year Eight when I first decided to ditch school for the day. I still remember it. A bunch of us headed to the local shopping mall. We thought we were true mavericks, hot on the trail of a new adventure. We just knew something incredible was going to happen. This was until we arrived at the mall and realised we had $5.60 between the five of us.

As a teacher now, I cannot stress the importance of consistent student attendance. Unfortunately, students think missing a class here and there will not have any dramatic effect on them. Statistics show differently. A student with an attendance percentage of 80% (missing one day a week) is equivalent to having missed one year's worth of schooling. The hard truth is, however, that once a student falls behind, it takes an incredible amount of work to catch back up, and unfortunately, once they are there, they will usually be left behind.

Still, the escapades can make for some enjoyable stories. Here are the highlights.

I barely ever leave campus grounds during break times these days. A decade ago, when I first came into the profession, most schools were still selling pies, sausage rolls, and an assortment of toasties as the prime pickings for nutrient sources. I would have to venture out to pick up something a little healthier. There was an opportunity cost involved in this decision, however, as most of the time, I would find myself having to complete copious amounts of paperwork in connection with the many students I would find attempting to skip school while on my way to and from the campus. I lost count of the number of times I pulled back into school grounds only to find a group of students truanting in the park right next to the school. Even better was when they would try to pull their school bags over their heads or run behind the closest tree in an attempt at disguising themselves. Numerous times I felt like walking over to the students and offering some advice. "We might need to apply a little thought here, team. Instead of all gathering in one spot, maybe let's put in a more coordinated effort, split up, and meet a few blocks away from the school." Instead, I called them over by name one-by-one and walked them single file up to the Deputy's office.

It seems like the mid-morning is the most common time for attempted student escapes from campus. Of all the different times over the years of arriving at work, this is when I seem to catch the most students attempting to skip school for the day. Just as I am about to pull my car into the surrounding neighbourhoods next to the school, I see student bodies start to appear. Nothing better than the look on students faces when they realise their day of adventure has now abruptly come to an end as I pull up slowly, telling them that, indeed, it is a shame that they have managed to become lost, but it is okay now as I will show them the way back. I then take on the role of a support vehicle, driving slowly behind the student/s till we make it back to school.

Students truanting in a country town were a little different. As the options for places for students to gather were limited, most students who would truant ended up hanging out outside the local shops, which all happened to be on the same street. Occasionally, I would use any free time I had at school to quickly run errands, heading into the centre of town. It was the reverse strategy of what I use in schools these days. If I see students truanting, I avoid being seen by them because if they caught me, they would come running up to tell me the adventures of their day so far. Then I had to reply, "Not trying to spoil your day here, team, but shouldn't you have been in my period two class this morning?"

Buddy Rooms

The buddy room can be an effective tool in behaviour management. To take a misbehaving student out from class and place them in another room to complete their work can provide the teacher and class a much-needed break. However, a few little details can change the use of this tool from effective to ineffective. Here are my tips.

Don't send students to rooms where their mates are. I imagine this sounds like common sense, but it is surprising over the years how many teachers continue to do this. Students rock up to their buddy room with a glint in their eyes and excitement in their hearts, noticing their friends in the room, envisioning the amount of chaos and carnage they are about to ignite. Due diligence is vital here! Find out which students are in the room before you start shipping new ones off.

Send a support person with the misbehaving student to make sure the student arrives at the desired location. I had a colleague who had an active student. The student was good-hearted. She just had a lot of energy. She was loud and had a master's degree in disruptive behaviour with the potential to pursue a Ph.D. I had an upper school class at the same time, so my colleague and I buddy roomed up, and I got to know this student quite well. Initially, my colleague would send the student to my class, but she would never turn up. My colleague then modified his plan and would send a support student with student X to my room to make sure she arrived. This worked for a time, but student X's popularity and power within the cohort saw her imposing her will on most support students, with the students making all kinds of excuses for her absence when they reached my door alone. The final play was to deliver student X to my class in a military-like formation with two students at the front, two students at the back, and Student X in the middle. The students and I couldn't help but laugh the first time this formation rocked up at my classroom door.

Setting the right environment for the buddy room is important. I have escorted students into some fascinating environments over my time. Here are a few.

At one school, a teacher made his senior school students sit in a circle around the student who had been taken to his class for misbehaving. The student who had been misbehaving would be placed in the middle with all eyes on them throughout the lesson. Usually, this environment is enough to deter a younger, lower school student from returning, but I did receive reports back one time that a student I had placed in the room took the experience by the horns and saw it as a chance to work on his comedy routine. He started lighting students up left, right, and centre till the whole room was in fits of laughter. We decided then and there it may not be the best place to send this student again.

In my first year, I was lucky enough to work with a dynamic, well-seasoned teacher. I had flutters of excitement run through my chest when I presented a student for buddy room time as I knew something out of left field would happen. Here are some of the better ones.

- If his Upper School students were sitting for a test, he would make the buddy room students sit for the test as well. Now, most students that had been sent to his class for misbehaving had no idea of the content, nor should they, as it was two to three years above their grade level. However, there were students that ended up doing quite well on the test. I was shut down quickly when I suggested maybe these students would be better off under the constant tutelage and supervision of this teacher.

- He made students teach his class. Not so he could slack off, but because he believed students sleeping at the back of the room were better than the disruption they were creating in their classrooms. "Students need to be held accountable for their actions."

One of the best strategies I have come across was between a pair of metalwork teachers. Any time they had a student misbehave, they sent the student with a note to the other teacher. The note would read, "Please ask teacher X for a long wait." The teacher receiving the note would make the student read the note aloud then disappear back into his workshop, while the remaining student would be left wondering when the teacher would return with the desired weight.

Finally, there must be a cap placed on the number of students sent out of class per period. If you start sending out too many students at once, the process becomes a game, and before you know it, you will have all kinds of ridiculous student behaviour just so they can get into the hall of fame. As enticing as it may seem to outsource the majority of your misbehaving students to various rooms around the school, you should restrict the buddy room process to only one or two students. I learned this the hard way. When I was completing my first practical experience, I had a tough year nine class. My mentor teacher had drilled it into me that consistency in behaviour management was the key to building a productive environment for this class. After I sent the fifth student in ten minutes out, she bounded up the corridor with a look of horror on her face and told me, "No more!"

I did ask later down the track if this was a new record for the school? There was no response.

Let's Get Ready to Rumble

Sometimes when I am walking the yard during duty, I think back to when I was in school and would hear the chant of, "Fight, fight, fight!" fly around. These days, it seems the spectacle of the fight, compared to the fight itself, is more compelling to students as images and reputations can be built or torn down during this time.

I guess I get it, though. For some students, it is a chance to establish themselves as a top dog or 'dogette' and for the school community to see the power they may or may not have. For others, it is a chance to defend themselves or knock down a bully, raising their own status, esteem, and confidence. Some just may not have received the regular thirteen hours of sleep that most teenagers are accustomed to and feel like someone must pay.

As a teacher, it is always interesting to see the strategising that goes into a school fight situation. Students fling around the school in droves, yelling to each other full of excitement and anticipation, pointing out the exact location of where and when it is to go down. I can't imagine many of them would make incredible jewel thieves with this level of lacking awareness, but they all know how to build some hype, that's for sure.

The same can be said for some teachers. In my initial years of teaching, I would have a little quiver of excitement run down my spine if I saw an impending altercation between students. I would launch myself headfirst into the ruckus, making sure to separate the parties involved while doing my best to restore some peace and order, all the while feeling like the champion of all things right in the world. I worked at one school where our department consisted of young, physically active males who liked a challenge. The school had an unofficial procedure for fights. If the fight was out of control, we would get the call up to head out and extinguish the flames. Being the first teacher on the scene became super competitive. Anything less, and you would be made to hear about it during Friday drinks. I swear, some stories of teachers stumbling or being slow of the mark stayed in the story cycle for a solid twelve months.

After the call came in, we would all scramble to launch out the door to head to the scene, splitting off into various roles once we arrived. A teacher or two would run into the centre of the student group. Another few teachers would be working the perimeter, continually calling out, "No more to see here," or, "Time to wrap it up, everyone. It is over." One of my favourite ones I used to hear was, "I wish you would all show this level of enthusiasm when you rock up to my class from now on." The final act was to escort the involved parties to a Deputy's office in administration. This could be a slight pain if you were all the way out on the oval and you had to bring the parties in from a distance, but we managed to make it work.

Meeting the Parents

It takes a village to raise a child. I had a student tell me once that back in their home country, they view teachers as their second parents. I felt like responding, "I just wish students here saw teachers as human beings."

Having students, parents, and teachers all working on the same page is genuinely a great thing. Unfortunately, more often than not, parental contact is for students misbehaving or doing the wrong thing. I taught a die-hard behaviourally challenged student once. What I mean is that in every class he was in, there would be problems. I made a note to myself early in the year to phone his home. I talked to his mother and told her that her son had been impressive in class during that particular week, which he had, and I was looking forward to the rest of the year. The mother was a tough character, and although she did her best to conceal it, I could tell she was happy for her son. For the remainder of the year, I would make phone calls home periodically and continue this process. The change in the student's belief in himself was remarkable. From little things, big things grow, I guess.

One of my favourite tricks for a misbehaving student is to find their parents' contact details on the school database and then, at one point during the lesson, call the student up to my desk and ask, "Just double-checking, are these the correct contact details for your parents?" How the students react to this will tell me a lot. Usually, the student has fallen into stunned silence, and it is a silent nod of the head as I dismiss the student back to the desk. Other times students start the negotiation process right then and there, telling me, "Sir, I promise I will be good from now on, just don't make the call."

Getting in contact with parents can be a little dubious. Not everyone has a phone, and even if they do, trying to find the right time to call can result in an endless game of phone tag. There has been an occasion or two where I have misread the contact details on the school database and phoned the wrong person. Only when I am halfway through the conversation does the voice remind me, "Sir, it is me (the student). We already had this conversation in class today." I apologise profusely then ask the student to pass the message on to their parents to get in contact with me. For some strange reason, this rarely seems to happen. Email is usually the easiest way to get in touch. Mind you, if I see the parent's email listed as something along the lines of luluhotpants@hotmail.com or beastslayer666@gmail.com, I start to reconsider whether it is worth it.

Having parents come in and meet face to face can be super beneficial, especially if it is a continual behaviour problem with a student. Most of the time, parents are great, and as long as they see their child is being treated fairly, they will be super supportive. I have received many great suggestions from parents as well. From, "No worries. If this continues, I will take the day off work and come sit next to you in class," to, "Well, it looks like that new fancy gaming console we just bought a few weeks ago is now going to have to be packed back up for a while." The most extreme case was when a mother bought a plane ticket for their child, who had been continually playing up in school. The mother told the child he would be heading back to his homeland for a couple of weeks to visit family. When they arrived at the airport, the mother turned to the child and told him it was actually a one-way ticket, and he would actually be staying there for a year as an incentive to clean his act up—which he did.

Parents can be very protective of their darling angels and are happy to jump down on anyone for any misdoings. Therefore, when I first contact a parent, I spend the initial minutes building the case slowly and in detail from the start, like a true law enforcement officer only dealing in facts. I have been in meetings with other teachers during which the first opportunity they had, they attacked the student, setting the parents off, leading to a war of words. For me, my objective is to present the situation as if I was in a court of law by using just the facts, reminding the parents that I know their angel isn't an evil person, and then offering a strategy or two about how we can improve from here. I have had the odd occasion in which a parent has seemed to want my head to roll from the very start of a meeting. I remind myself to stay composed. By the time I have finished setting the scene, the parent has often done a complete 180-degree turn, realising that their darling angel may not have been telling them the truth about the situation.

Saying Goodbye to Sir, Yes, Sir

A quiet, orderly room with students on task and being productive. This is how I used to measure the success of my lessons. There are still days where I strive for this, but I am a lot more lenient than I once was. I am still big on routine, discipline, and organisation... I just remind myself that I am preparing students for life beyond school, not advancing into hostile territory. So, I hone my skills accordingly.

During my initial years, I used to set up my classroom at the start of every year with students' desks individually spaced out to ensure minimal distraction and interruption between students. Student Collaborative Learning was prominent during this time, and schools across the state were being directed down this path. The idea was to create groups with a mixture of student ability levels, having students work together to help each other grow in their learning. These days, I am all for it. Especially with screen usage being so high, it is excellent for students to be able to put down their devices and communicate with one another in a safe, educational environment. In my first years, it turned into more of a behaviour management nightmare than a success story in group learning. Students were more than happy to communicate with one another; unfortunately, it was about anything except the assigned task. Sharing time was amusing. After a set time, student groups had to discuss their findings with the class. Most groups' spokespeople felt that if they admitted that they had not completed the task and stood at the front of the class long enough staring off into the distance, I would feel sorry for them, and this would be enough for me to turn to the next group. Unfortunately for the students, I saw this as a life teaching moment and reminded them that it was essential to finish anything you start in life. Some of the creative insight that came out of students' mouths from this point on was fascinating.

My short-felt success, unfortunately, came to an end when I moved to another school. The new school had a lot of disciplinary problems. Students weren't overly impressed with my approach and would tell me so continually in a not-so-formal manner. I was still young, naive, and stubborn, so I continued down this path for a while longer but eventually had the epiphany that maybe I needed to loosen the reins a little and trust the class a bit more. Although not a ground-breaking strategy that led to increased productivity, our classroom environment was a lot more positive, and my rapport with students grew so much stronger.

These days, I am more relaxed in my approach. It has almost been a complete reversal. My students are seated in groups, and we consistently complete pair and group activities, which the students seem to enjoy. There are times I still become frustrated when students are off-task or try to carry on with their conversations, but I don't let it get to me. In the past, I would have seen this as a personal attack on me and my ability to control a class, but now I simply remind myself that not every learning activity will be incredibly gripping for every student and that continual reflection and professional growth is a good thing.

It was hard dialling down my militant way. It felt like I was giving over my control, and that scared me. I still provide a disciplined and organised learning place, but I now meet the students halfway and buckle in for the ride.

Smoking de Herb

I have only caught students using drugs a handful of times. The majority of these times, it was smoking marijuana. The tricky part is when I can't catch the students red-handed, but all my senses tell me they are as high as a kite. With all the cover-up tools young people have access to these days, and most students knowing that all they must do is never admit to anything, it is becoming increasingly hard to prove any wrongdoing. One of my favourite strategies if I suspect a student or usually a group of students is high is to stop the lesson midway through and start talking in detail about all my favourite comfort foods out of the blue. I will spend a few minutes brainstorming the reasons why I like certain foods and then pass it over to the students for their input, making sure I maintain a straight face throughout. Watching the students' eyes becoming increasingly shifty to avoid eye contact and doing their best not to giggle or show an abnormal amount of intrigue always makes for a fun few minutes, at least for me anyway. I was teaching a year eleven class some time ago. It was only a small class of all male students. Most of the lessons were after lunch or recess. They would all enter the room in a zombie-like state, find their chair to sit down and start staring at a different random piece of the wall, doing their best not to cross eyes with anyone. Some even forgot to close their mouths. In one lesson, I had just finished the direct instruction component and was about to pass it over to the students for independent practice. Instead, I burst into a monologue on my favourite European baked desserts, and the room came alive. I let it go for a few minutes, then posed the question to the class, "Any particular reason we are so excited about food right now, fellas?" The room once again fell into a deathly silence.

I have also noticed that students who tend to participate in these types of behaviours can be super creative in the kitchen. These talents have been on display on more than one occasion when I just happened to be walking past a home economics room and looked in. The only problem is when the students see me looking in and then offer me some of their food. I find myself in a catch twenty-two. If I say yes, I am pretty sure they haven't added any of their 'special ingredients' to the mix, but then again, I have a lesson next period, and what if they have? Can I afford to spend the rest of the day wrestling with my mind in the grips of paranoia? If I say no, I could possibly shut the student down and all the hard work we have done building up trust is now back to square one. Once again, I find myself walking the fine line.

The One-Percenters

When I played football, every coach I ever had would always talk about the *'one-percenters.'* These are the little important things that we can do as teammates for one another. They may not necessarily get the same recognition as the snap kick goal from the boundary line or the mark that saw a teammate leap on someone's back, but nevertheless, they are equally as important. The crux is, if we all do the little things the *one-percenters* do, it will start to have a compounding effect over time and will lead to a healthy environment and successful team.

I have tried to implement this philosophy into my classroom practice, especially when working with student behaviour. I tell students we do the *one-percenters* like pushing our chair in when leaving class, making sure any rubbish goes into the bin, arriving to class on time, having the respect to listen to one another when your classmate is speaking, and creating an environment where learning through failure is encouraged rather than judged. This will help you and the people around you grow.

When I talk about the *one-percenters* for negative student behaviour, I am not talking about the student who tells you to, "Get fu&$ed," because you asked him or her for their answer to question two. Or the student who has been eyeballing you since the start of the lesson looking for a confrontation. The *one-percenters* are those low-key student behaviours that, when they first occur, you consider them more of a minor irritation than lesson-stopping power plays. But if they go unchecked, they can start to build into their own negative force and destroy the classroom environment.

These are the typical low-key behaviours from students that drive me insane:

Students have an uncanny ability to see their time as more precious than others' in the class, especially that of the teacher. The number of times over the years where I have had students rock up to class directly after lunch and ask to go to the toilet or get a drink is incredible. I always find it interesting pursuing the case a little further and asking them why they couldn't accomplish this task during lunchtime. Most of the time, the response is, "I didn't want to waste my break." At least honesty is still a thing.

I am big on organisation. It has worked for me and my chaotic ways over the years. I always greet the students at the beginning of the lesson as they walk through the door, giving them a few instructions. Take your textbook out, turn to such and such page, and finally, I rifle off the resources needed for the lesson. Usually, none of the students have them. Still, to this day, the amount of time students can waste just by sitting there, as if making it into the class was their significant accomplishment for the day, still astounds me. Or the fellas entering class who feel the need to shake everyone's hand, even though they had just spent most of the lunch together and possibly every previous period.

Background murmuring when I am speaking drives me crazy. Sure, it is disrespectful, but most of the time, the student speaking is going to be the one that asks me, "What are we doing now, Sir?" as soon as I finish speaking. I have found if you can stomp out this behaviour early, students catch on pretty quick. Another annoyance is the student you can see staring off into space with their mouth wide open as you are explaining in detail everything that is needed. Then, as you finish, that student pipes up with, "Sir, just double-checking…" I have even had the occasional student fall asleep in my class. In these situations, I like to get the room as quiet as possible, then watch the student awaken with all the other students' eyes now on them.

Three Strikes and I Am Out

Year Nine was an all-star calibre year for me. Hormones were in full effect, a flourishing mental disorder (that I kept to myself and only my family knew about), and I had a mouth that once let loose was hard to reel back, and that landed me in all kinds of trouble. These are some of those times.

I once racked up a seventy-three-minute detention during a single science lesson. Not trying to brag, just more impressed that the teacher went the distance. It was still early in the year, but the teacher and I had become well acquainted, and it was fair to say there was no mutual admiration between us. I look back now and realize he wasn't a bad guy, just coming to school to get paid. Sure, a concept here and there would be taught, but nothing too over the top. The class was crazy. I don't want to paint the wrong picture here. In no way was I an innocent bystander, but I wasn't just misbehaving as a lone wolf either. More like I was feeding my competitive soul. Once other students laid down some of their best work early on, I knew I had to elevate my game.

One day, the teacher told me that for every time I misbehaved, a single stroke would be placed on the blackboard to signify one minute of detention after school. After receiving my tenth stroke in four minutes, my form was too hot, and I knew I had to fully commit to see where this would take me. Seventy-three minutes was the final destination. The final bell went, and there I was, sitting in silence as the teacher erased three of my minute markers. The next thing I knew, one of the football coaches from our school was whisking me away, telling my science teacher that I was needed as a local news station was doing a segment on the upcoming state-wide school football competition. As I was one of the captains, I was required to attend. It was all a little surreal, walking out of the class to see seventy single markers remaining on the blackboard, then fifteen minutes later being in front of the cameras.

During the same year, I spent three months (on and off) in school isolation. Since my start as a teacher, I no longer see these rooms in operation, which is good as they were soul-destroying. Truanting from school, fighting in school, and general misconduct in class was what landed me in timeout for stints at a time. The room was set up in the back of the stage area with six to eight cubicles all spaced out so you couldn't see each other. When school started for the day, you had to report to the stage area to begin your isolation time. I would be in there for the entire day and was not allowed to do anything: no schoolwork, nothing. Just stare at the wall in front for a few hours, have a break for recess and lunch, then get back to it. Teachers would rotate through each period, and some were more professional than others. One time I managed to sneak in my audio device and had it playing sneakily through my jumper arm; next rotation, this was found and taken away. By the end of the day, I had lost my disc-man, a pack of cards, a slinky, and a mini skateboard (the one you could work with your fingers and do tricks).

I am the only person to this day from the school to get a red card while being a waterboy during an Upper School girls' football match. Again, not boasting about this, just highlighting that year nine may not have been my best year. One of our players had been hit high (rough behind play), and the umpire had not called it. It's probably worth mentioning that the umpire was also the coach from the school we were playing at the time. I took umbrage to this and told the umpire exactly what had happened as it had happened right next to me. When he denied it, I told him everything that was wrong with his life and continued to do this for a further two to three minutes until he showed me the yellow card, then finally the red card.

Working It Out

I spent two years of my career being too stubborn to change my ways in behaviour management. I was already five or six years in at this point, and I told myself I knew it all. Usually, as a class, we would get through to the other side and end in the right place, but there was a student/class that forever remained in the fire of combat.

I wondered, when I saw teachers fighting the same battles with students day in and day out with no sense of change or improvement, why they stay in the industry? Why wake up each morning hating what you do, counting down the moments till the day is over? Life is too short, and being a teacher is too important of a position to be grinding away like that day after day. But I guess I can see it now. As teachers, we all have a sense of pride and feel that our varying levels of experience should make us exempt from dealing with these disruptive situations anymore.

Anyway, the following is a list of mistakes I have made and witnessed other colleagues make that will affect your class's rapport.

Demanding vs. Earning respect: Respect must be earned. As a teacher, you need to be in the trenches with the students and go through the ups and downs. Just because you are older, have a degree, industry experience, or have raised your own children, doesn't automatically qualify you as the most respected figure in the room.

Firm but Fair: Don't be the teaching tool that wants to be every student's best friend. Sure, this may feel good initially, make up for some inability or social gap you experienced when you were back in the day, but it is lame. Be firm but fair. Be the adult in the room and lead by example for future generations. Show students you care, but you will hold them accountable for their actions. The most important thing is to be consistent in your efforts.

The Power Struggle: How students are viewed by their peers during their time in high school can be detrimental to their daily wellbeing. Reputations are formed, friendships are aligned, and a student's place in the school community will start to be shaped or solidified. Entering the power struggle is a dangerous place for a teacher. If the situation doesn't break the way they were hoping, they will lose face in front of their class, and their reputation will pay the price. This is not to say that teachers should avoid this zone entirely, as there will be times that will require you to make a stand. However, if you do enter this zone, you want to make sure you know what you want to achieve. Adolescents want to test you. Just see it as their psychological and emotional right of passage.

Winning Students Over: If a student likes you, they will learn from you. Even better, if a student believes you genuinely care for them, the sky can be the limit for their personal growth. Small pieces of detailed praise when a student has persevered or overcome adversity, no matter how small, is a powerful tool—no need to go overboard as students will be able to sniff out any exaggeration. Just quick, concise feedback to let the student know they have done a good job, you appreciate their perseverance, and that they are in control of their life.

Judging a Book by its Cover: No one likes being known as the anti-social type, the rough and tumble character, the no-good one. Everyone has a story, and those stories can force students to take on a certain character, and at times build not-so-pleasant reputations for themselves. As teachers, we can help these students break this feedback loop. Sure, you will be let down over time, and it may be more than once—but the students you help to overcome their self-limitations will remind you why you took up the job in the first place.

More Than Curriculum

Quality education needs to be based on more than just building a student's knowledge of the curriculum. Building self-worth, resilience, social skills, and personal interests are all equally important and require attention.

With everything happening during a teaching day, it can be hard to touch on these skills regularly. Other times I have had to remind myself that even though my lesson may be heading downhill, there is still time to salvage something, and I will switch to focus on a life skill for the remainder of the lesson.

Here are some of the skills I focus on:

Resilience: People hate to fail, and even worse, people hate to fail in a public setting. Building in processes by which students are allowed to fail in a safe environment is a powerful thing. It is important to model this as a teacher. Any time I make a mistake (which is often), I don't get flustered. Instead, I thank the student for pointing it out and continue on my way. Suppose a shy student or a student who does not normally participate in whole-class discussions overcomes their fear and attempts the work. In that case, I make sure to note this in front of the class—nothing overboard, just an acknowledgement that I understand what you have just overcome. Let's continue down this path.

Connection: Walking around during break times these days, I am more likely to see a bunch of students huddled together all on their individual screens with minimal talk than students talking eye-to-eye. This struck home recently when, after I had my students complete an assessment, I gave them a five-minute break to step outside the room. When I went to call them in moments later, eleven students were standing next to each other just outside our classroom door, all on their screens with no one speaking. Recently I have made an effort to designate five to ten minutes at the end of each lesson to generate class discussions on the happenings in the world. This may mean I need to stay informed with current trends in celebrity romances, popular console games, and possible trade situations in various sporting leagues, but it gives students a chance to open up verbally and work on a skill other than what is included in the school curriculum.

Time Management and Organisation: Nothing frustrates me more than a student turning up late to class and just taking up their seat with no explanation. I am not talking about the student who slides into class a few minutes late with a cheeky grin on their face, but the student who is a good ten to fifteen minutes late with a look on their face that symbolises, "Didn't you know my time is more important than yours?" Keeping this student accountable every time and using positive reinforcement of even the slightest change towards arriving on time can help this student start to shave time off.

The Minimalist: This is the name I give to students who only bring the bare essentials to class. Over the years, this standard has dropped significantly, with students these days arriving to class with nothing but themselves, expecting that they have hit the standard. The example I like to use with my students is to imagine you are a tradesperson, and I call you to complete some work at my house. After I have finished explaining the job, you ask to borrow my tools as you didn't think to bring yours.

Manners: I am not expecting students to bow or curtsy when I walk into the room (although this would be incredible), but students waving their hands and clicking their fingers expecting me to drop everything and attend to their every want is not the way to approach it. A simple, quick conversation with a student reminding them that I am their teacher, not servant as well as pointing out, "See all these other students' hands currently raised in the air? I promise I will get to you, just not the second you want my attention," will set this student straight.

Accountability: "You are in charge of your life, young people! I am here to help, and I want to support you in your growth, but you will learn the most about yourself by working through your challenges and keeping yourself honest and accountable."

To be able to incorporate life skills into lessons on a daily basis would be great for a student's holistic growth. Unfortunately, those curriculum points can be stubborn and require an immense amount of planning and detail to achieve.

Boys Will Be Boys

"We are going to stay up all night, and it is going to be crazy fun!" a group of male students spoke aloud a few rows back from where I was seated before exploding into fits of excitement. I remember thinking to myself, we were only ninety minutes into our ten-hour bus ride, and I was already reconsidering whether I was going to make it. My next train of thought was, I had barely managed to look after myself for the previous twenty-four years; how was I now supposed to be responsible for fifty Year Eight students for seven days and nights? Not that the students needed to know that.

It was 2010, and I was working in the country. I had taken on the role of Year Eight coordinator (my first time in this role). We sat around at a meeting at the start of the year as a pastoral care team for the school, trying to strengthen student wellbeing. It was somehow decided that a week-long camp would be a great transition event (back then, this was the first year of high school). I must admit I was a little bitter that my idea of a mid-morning sausage sizzle followed by a round-robin basketball competition was shot down so quickly. This was mostly because all the teachers who had suggested the camp were not the ones going along. In fact, we were the only year group going to camp. Tricks of the seasoned teacher, I tells ya.

The handy thing with teaching in the country is the abundance of prime locations to choose from. I remember when I was in school, we would head out an hour from the city, pitch a tent on a sand mound somewhere and hope that the deck of cards we had and our creativity would see us through the next five days.

The remainder of the bus journey can be summed up with these key points:
- Reading and individual 'quiet time' is not the go-to option for most twelve to thirteen-year-olds. I am sure I heard one song repeated twenty or thirty times throughout our journey. I imagined it is what the descent into hell must feel like.
- One student asked me close to one hundred questions over a fifteen-minute period. They were not trying to break a record or

be annoying, just genuinely curious about my life outside the classroom. Five minutes after our conversation ended, I looked back around to find my new mate passed out with his head on the window—too much thinking for the little guy.

- Another male student decided to mark the midway point of the journey with a celebratory dance. His dance's only problem involved dropping his pants and flashing his rear end at another driver out the window. The situation became even more tricky when his two friends caught him by surprise and closed the window on him from each end, leaving him and his rear backside hanging out the window. I would like to say you should have seen the look on the driver's face, but I was too busy trying to figure out how best to handle this situation.

- Young people loaded up on sugar produce a whirlwind of emotions.

Setting up camp is always interesting. We were all staying in tents, and luckily enough, the campground provided the tents. Students working in small groups were now responsible for getting their shelter up. Straight away, the rat pack of boys swooped up their tent and headed to the furthest boundary. Another group of lads followed close behind. When I looked over, I saw that the females were going about it a little differently. Most of them were sitting on their tent canvas, refusing to move. When I enquired what was happening, they replied that they were waiting to speak to management as they felt their work conditions were unfavourable. I told them they had thirty minutes to get their tents up, or they would be sleeping with the kangaroos.

No camp would be complete without a late-night escape attempt. This great escapade was to take place during the second night. I knew this as I would be heading somewhere and randomly stumble across small pockets of students discussing the logistics in great detail throughout the day. Most of the time, I would just hear, "Yeah, we are in," before I appeared, and suddenly all conversation would shut up shop. When the night rolled around, it turned out to be a little uneventful. Having now repositioned my own tent in the middle of 'escape headquarters,' their attempts were futile though hilarious. Most played the usual routine of waiting for me to fall asleep then shoot their shot at escape. Their faces in the spotlight of my torch every time they tried to unzip their tent were priceless.

By far, the most bizarre event I encountered was the amount of time the boys spent putting into their hair and outfit for bed each night. One hour before bed, I would start sending the students off in droves to the solitary bathroom block to start getting ready for bed. With fifteen minutes to go, I would head over and hurry along with any stragglers. Thinking there would only be a handful of students left, I was surprised to see half the fellas wearing collared shirts and applying hair gel. I did announce to them it was a little unlikely that they would find the love of their life in the fifty-metre walk from the ablution block to their tent, so maybe the gel and effort would not be needed for the remainder of our stay.

Double Trouble

Country Week is always a big deal for students in rural regions. Country schools send sporting teams to the city the last week of term two. Most schools send at least one or two teams to compete in a range of team sports. The week attracts all types of characters: the ultra-competitive students, the students who just want to give their selected sport a go, and the students who are incredibly eager to head to the city and go on a shopping spree.

It was my second year taking a team down, and altogether we had about fifty students across six teams representing our school. I was coaching the Senior boys' volleyball team. We had started training earlier than usual, and the team was coming together nicely heading into the week.

'*Double Trouble*' became known to me three weeks out from the tournament. Coaches must send around a list of names of the students who will be competing. Students' criteria to attend is they must be up to date with all their assessments, and their behaviour in class has to have been reasonable. Teachers of these students then agree or disagree whether the student will be able to attend. Most of the time, teachers see the bigger picture. It is a chance for students to head away and have experiences beyond the classroom—possibly the opportunity to excel at something. Double Trouble were two big lads. They were good fellows but not overly inspired by the day-to-day happenings of the classroom. Their forms came back, and straight away, I had to start getting myself into negotiation mode. With a little back and forth, I managed to get each teacher's approval as long as Double Trouble completed all the work they owed by the time we were to leave. I ended up spending about a week and a half with these lads till 6 pm most nights, making sure they were all caught up. I had forgotten how intriguing the topic of photosynthesis could be.

We went through the qualifying rounds, only dropping one set in all our games. The boys really looked like they were enjoying themselves. Double Trouble stepped up to the plate and delivered. They dived for loose balls, provided never-ending support for their teammates, and showed a level of maturity and poise that made them both leaders on the court. In between games, we headed out and watched other teams from our schools compete. This is when Double Trouble indeed came alive. I remember heading out as a group to watch the girls' soccer game. We were perched up on a hill with one half of Double Trouble sitting at the top of the hill, a little off to the side. I didn't understand why the second half burst out laughing before calling out, "Launching cannon number one!" Then, number one took off rolling down the hill. Not the usual way of rolling arm over arm either. It was the more dramatic head over shoulder, making sure to land perfectly at the feet of two girls who were passing by. The girls stopped in amusement as number one calmly stared up at them, proclaiming, "Your beauty has made me fall head over heels for you," the girls managing a smirk as they had witnessed his tumble from the top.

There were several night-time activities throughout the week. With dinners, movies, and game theatres, the students were never starving for action. One night we returned to our hotel. It was towards the end of the trip. The other coaches and I had retired to our rooms for about an hour before it had been reported that students had been mooning (flashing their backsides) at patrons in the hotel across the street. Our head teacher had become hysterical and summoned all the coaches to head down to check on their teams. As we weren't the only school in the hotel, I was hoping it would not be my lads. I picked up my room key and headed downstairs. Entering the door, I could see six figures lurking behind the curtain on the outside terrace. I silently made my way out towards them. I could hear them yelling and cheering, and a few were counting. When I pulled the curtain back, I could see most of the boys on the terrace stunned to see me. I looked over to find my missing team member (one half of Double Trouble) hanging from a pole in between the two rooms with nothing but ten floors of free-falling to the ground if he let go. Apparently, his recent effort of holding on had made him the new record holder, although I was quick to pull him in. After a stern talking-to, I turned and headed away. I kept wrestling with the idea in my head. I didn't know if I was more terrified by the act or impressed by the athleticism of the feat.

The Night of Broken Dreams and Promises

"The night of broken dreams and promises" is how a teacher once described Parent Night to me. Don't get me wrong; I am sure he was once full of joy and optimism, just experienced one too many of these nights. I hope, anyway.

Usually, you have taught every period, and if you were super lucky, you had year nines last period and were able to reacquaint yourself with some of your favourite self-soothing techniques. You tell yourself mid-lesson that you are growing as a person. However, you do have building doubt that maybe you had to be insane to sign up for this profession. There is usually an hour or so break after your final class of the day before parents start to file through the door. You make your way down fifteen-twenty minutes before your first appointment. The first task to complete is to arrange your office for the evening (a desk from a classroom). The aim is to have everything laid out in just a way that suggests you are a professional, but not so much as to entice endless questions where speaking may prove otherwise. I always seem to have a stack of lined paper nearby that never gets used.

Working in mathematics, the appointments are always full and last from start to finish of the time slot. There is a five to seven-minute window for each parent. Sticking to these time frames is crucial. Too little, and you leave parents doubting your professional ability or dedication, and too long, you spend your time re-answering the same questions in what now has become somewhat of a compulsive ritual.

I enjoy listening to my colleagues around me if I have a quick break. Most teachers are down the line offering information on difficulties experienced and ways for students to improve. However, there is always one colleague in the room who starts going off on a tangent, promising Heaven and Earth, sometimes even the path to complete transcendency if they get the chance. I find this amusing as it usually comes from the colleague who is routinely late to class, has left campus by 3:12 p.m. most days, and offers radical suggestions for student improvement at staff meetings, yet can't be found when actions are required.

If dad is present, it is his chance to tell me how much he excelled at mathematics in his day, which is incredibly convenient as there is no way to complete a quick fact check on this. If he is there with his son, he throws it in his face and tells him to lift his game, but if it is his daughter, he will say to her, she still has time to grow into her best mathematical self. Usually, mum will tell me how much she disliked maths growing up or that she was okay with it until the day algebra started showing up.

The night ends with me walking to my car, absolutely drained. I will usually awake suddenly from my slumber a few hours later, remembering everything I now need to do to make sure I haven't just turned the occasion into a night of broken dreams and promises.

Playing for Keeps

There was a bit of a lead-up to this event. We were about halfway through term one when it was announced that the students would square off against the teachers in a football match. As part of their work experience, a few Senior School students were organising the event, with all proceeds going to charity. I was teaching the leading student in charge of organising the event at the time, and although mathematics was not his favourite time of the day, he did have a few notable claims to fame. He was the last student to have put the school into lockdown. A student from another local high school had come looking for him during school hours, armed with weapons. He had also single-handedly brought down after-school detentions at our school, although he didn't elaborate on that one. Still being early in the year and not knowing him that well, I didn't know how to take him. Pretty much every lesson for the weeks leading up to the game, he would tell me in detail how he was going to take me out during the game or how he had been selected for the under 16's stateside, and his skills would be too slick for me. Usually, when a student starts talking brashly, they run out of comments, or their confidence in their stories starts to waver, and this is their tell for me to know that they are just talking it up. This was different; it just kept on going.

To be honest, I had not applied a whole heap of thought to the event. Even that day, it remained only in the background of my mind. The one thing I do remember thinking was, I had year eights last period, and I wondered how pumped up they were going to be after watching the game. Would my planned lesson on Pythagoras' Theorem prove to be as life-changing as I had envisioned? Should I just consider a career change and start teaching physical education, so these days would always be my lessons? As I walked onto the ground to take my place, my final thought was, how is this going to work with no tackling? Is this all just for show to prove that teachers and students can work together?

I knew this was no expedition match from the first bounce, and we would be playing for keeps. As soon as the ball hit the ground, one of the sports teachers flew in and nailed a student in a tackle. A few moments later, a student made a decent bump into one of the teachers, and my mind soon went from teachers vs. students to prisoners vs. guards. Don't get me wrong; the game was played in excellent spirits; it just had an element of brute physicality. That and no teacher can stand hearing a student go on about their victory for the weeks to come.

My student, who had been talking brashly for weeks leading up to the game, had gone missing early on after a decent tackle had been laid on him by one of the female teachers. He had moved into the forward line soon after, and when he had the chance to kick a goal ten metres out directly in front, he missed everything. It was at this time I started to question the truth of his previous week's statements. Either that or the state team's selection criteria these days was a lot lower than I had anticipated.

The teachers ended up winning convincingly. It does help when you have fully matured bodies, and three-quarters of the team had played a high-level competitive sport during one point in their lives. Still, a win is a win, and you must let people know about it. Especially the students.

The aftermath was interesting. The next day we had a schoolwide meeting that had been scheduled previously. Watching the teachers limp through the door one by one, reminiscing on varying degrees of battle from the match, definitely helped motivate me to push through the next ninety minutes. The principal started the meeting with, "Well done to everyone who participated yesterday. It was great to see. Going into the match, I thought it might be necessary to talk to the students before the game about what is expected. Having watched the match, I now know it was the teachers I should have talked to beforehand." I am pretty sure he was joking. I hope.

Finally, my overconfident student had taken a few days of absence after the game. His demeanour on return was priceless! His slouch posture said it all, and although he did try to offer up an excuse here and there for his lack of performance, he did congratulate me on a good game. A few of the teachers had managed to gather many brochures from the local gym close to the school. For a solid two weeks after the game, we made our way around the school during recess and lunch time, handing out the brochures to students we had played against, suggesting this was the extra work that would be needed if they were to challenge us next year. Every little bit counts.

Water Park Madness

Heading to the local water park at the end of the year for a 'day out' was something that the students always looked forward to. I didn't realise it would be the teachers who took centre stage on this one.

The day was seen as a reward activity for students. If you had attended class and been doing the right thing, like trying to learn, you qualified for a discounted admission rate to the park. The setup was pretty simple. As soon as students entered the park, they were on their own, and teachers would be walking around to 'supervise.' Did this mean catching up on sleep, sun tanning, and reading the paper? Sure, all were part of the supervisory role.

It was my first year at a new school back in the city, and I didn't know what to expect. I had my bag packed and loaded up with way more survival supplies than needed and checked myself in. There was a public announcement from the headteacher to commence the day. Then, he took up his chair and unfolded his paper, the signal that the day had begun. I was swooped up by a gang of teachers and headed towards the go-carts. As soon as we were in, it was carnage. No waiting for the go light. It was on smashing into each other, taking no prisoners, and making sure to trash talk anyone who fell behind.

Leaving the go-carts, it was then onto the speed slides. Being a young male teacher, I am always aware of my position as a role model. However, when I was at the top of the slides, ready to launch, it was all about the win, no matter the cost. The manipulation of body parts from the other teachers to gain any extra speed was fascinating and of course, one time through was not enough. Each time waiting in the line, a new student would pop up his or her head offering a new area of thought as to why they could win, only to be proven wrong.

The highlight of the day was the rapids. Armed with a tube tyre, it was off down the shoot, or at least I thought. Again, leading by example, students were tipped off their tubes, waterways were blocked for minutes, and I swear my nose dived into the cement on the floor a good ten times. After some time running these antics, the lifeguards had to get involved, which was an interesting dynamic to see a young, lowly-paid employee trying to discipline a slightly older, slightly higher-paid group of teachers. When the day was done, I headed off, leaving behind all the carnage of the day.

"Oh, I Get It. You Do It for the Holidays."

Recently, a collection of memes circulated on social media, comparing what people actually do at their jobs in contrast to what people think they do. I did not come across the set for teaching, although I am sure there are some out there. Below are several common misconceptions of teachers I have experienced from non-teaching folk.

Holidays: The most prominent one of all. I once trained with a gentleman who loved to bring up the number of holidays I get as a teacher. At first, it started as an awkward joke, "Mate, it's two weeks into the term. You must be on holiday soon." I laughed at first as I thought he would have enough common sense to understand what teachers work through during the term and the need for holidays to recharge motivation, patience, and all-around social prowess. I did think to remind him of this but then reassured myself it would only be a short-lived thing. It wasn't. Eventually, my need to set him straight outweighed my desire to support his emotional and social growth through this period. So, I laid it on him, telling him that he was more than welcome to follow me around for a day as I taught, then he may understand the need for holidays after ten weeks of day in and day out interactions with young people, staring directly into his soul as I spoke. His jokes have since come to a halt.

I am not saying that the number of holidays teachers receive during the year is not an attractive incentive to head into the career, but it is not always what it seems. This is typically how my holidays go. For the short ones, the two weeks between terms, I spend the first two to three days crashed on a couch somewhere. I am still surprised how, with ten years in the game, my body and mind always go through this. By the end of the first week, I am out living large and experiencing the good life. By the time the start of the second week rolls around, I am back in my home office, using most mornings to get my planning done for the coming term.

Anyone can do it: Those who can, do, those who cannot teach. This statement drives me insane and, judging by the large dropout rate from teaching in the early years, is completely untrue. I am not going to launch into everything that teachers do during a given day and the different roles they take on, but I will say teachers deserve more respect and that a teacher who is good at what they do is a valuable thing and needs to be seen as such.

We have fun all day: I was asked by a non-teaching acquaintance once, do you ever get bored of having fun all day? I didn't know what she meant, so I asked, "As in helping students overcome their self-limitations and become better versions of themselves?" She genuinely responded, "No, as in going into school and just hanging out with students all day." I was absolutely gobsmacked.

Students always master things the first time you teach them: "Just get them to copy down the steps from the whiteboard and then explain it to them." This is another profound statement a non-teaching folk once exclaimed to me when his wife had asked me out of the blue what my thoughts were on students and different learning styles. All students do not learn the same way, nor do all students understand everything at the same pace—and thank God for that as otherwise there would be no need for struggle, and deeper understanding would not occur.

How students behave in class is a reflection of the teacher: Sure, there can be some truth to this, and it is true that personalities definitely do clash in a classroom. However, how a student is moulded at home is equally as important. High schools are a unique environment for this with all the hormones, mental health issues, and uncertainty going on during that period. By no means am I taking shots at parents, just stating that there is more that goes into building a person than their four hours of Mathematics classes per week.

Being a Graduate Teacher

While completing my Diploma of Education, I first read the statistic that fifty percent of teachers walk away from the profession within the first five years. I saw this as a challenge—a badge of honour if I could last it out. In my mind, I thought I was prepared, but it was different once I started actually doing it.

Below are some survival tips that helped me during my first years in the profession.

Learn to say no: When I first started out, I was young and eager and wanted to throw myself into everything possible. Although initially, it felt great that I was involved in most things, over time, it got the best of me. In teaching, one of our most important resources is time, and unfortunately, it can be whittled away quickly. Mastering the skill of saying no will repay itself tenfold throughout the rest of your career. It doesn't need to be a blanket no to everything; just pick and choose and look after yourself where possible.

Don't smile till Easter: An excellent seasoned teacher told me this. It wasn't until I had transitioned from the graduate teacher phase, but it is an excellent piece of advice I now pass onto any teacher about to start in the profession. Students want to test boundaries and even your character at times. If you remain disciplined in being firm but fair for the entire first term, students will understand that you are no walkover, but at the same time, you care about them and their progress. They will learn to trust you.

Keep records of any positive feedback flowing your way: It is easy to think the world hates you and you are in the wrong profession when you hear, "Get fu'ked, Sir. I f'ing hate you," for the third time in a day. There were plenty of times I would walk out of classes and into the office, making sure no one was around, and start headbutting a nearby wall, softly questioning everything I was doing. It doesn't need to be this way. I attended a Professional Development Day for graduate teachers in my first year. The person running the seminar mentioned that back in the days when he was in the classroom, he would keep a box of any positive feedback he had received. It may be in the form of letters, printed emails, or merely remembering to write down any good thing students would pass on to him. I started collecting later that year, and I make sure to have the container close by when I have days that may not have been overly flattering.

Break down the term: It's easy to look at the calendar after a lousy lesson early in the term and start to curse to yourself, realising how much of the term remains. Hell, I have even witnessed teachers swear out loud about this. I work in two-week blocks. I write down everything I want to achieve by the end of those two weeks. I then do a quick reflection when I get there. Nothing crazy, just little reminders that I am on the right path, and the end is always moving closer.

Don't make teaching everything in your life: Balance is a good thing. We are in classrooms day in and day out, and it is mentally and emotionally draining. It is easy to hang behind after school, putting in the hours to prepare the perfect lessons for the next day, but this will soon become overwhelming. One of the best pieces of advice I was given during my graduate days was to set myself a departure time every day. I had to promise myself that no matter how my day had gone or where I was up to in my planning, I had to leave at this time. The extra and important detail was that once I left the office, whatever had happened at school that day was now behind me. Now, this is a discipline and will take a while to get used to, but it is well worth it.

Side Effects of Teaching
I love what I do for a profession, but geez, it has aged me early!

When I was an adolescent, I would get into my mother's car to head to sports training most days after school. Usually, my training sessions were just after when mum had arrived home from teaching, so I had to prepare myself before entering the car as the radio volume would be sky-high. I remember thinking to myself, how is it even possible to listen to anything at this high of a level? Then I started teaching, and it became crystal clear. Working in a classroom with thirty students for an hour at a time, your hearing will begin to dissipate. I now know this when my partner happens to get into my car after just having arrived home from school. She will lean over to lay one on me (give me a kiss) before jumping out of her seat in shock and terror when I turn the radio back on.

Over my career, I have learned to realign my expectations with reality. When I started in the profession, I envisioned every lesson being earth-shatteringly good. Students would have no other choice but to rise to their feet and applaud to show their appreciation. This has never once happened, and it was a steep learning curve. These days, if I can get a student to find a pen and write their name on their page within the first ten minutes of class, I chalk up a 'W' in the win column. There was a graduate teacher I worked with once. She was in her first year of teaching. The first few weeks of the year, she was full of positivity and good intentions. I had seen this many times before, so I made a quick mental note to check back in on her towards the end of the term. Sure enough, on the last day of term, I just happened to be walking into our office to retrieve a resource when I noticed the teacher (no one else was in the office at the time) slumped in her chair with her head in her hands and a posture that had defeat written all over it. When I asked her what was wrong, she simply replied, "Teaching has bamboozled me." Fortunately, she picked herself up and turned into an excellent teacher, but there are always those 'what if' moments.

My tolerance level for being taught by someone else is incredibly low. When my partner and I first acquired our new puppy, we thought it would be a good idea to get him trained while he was still young, so it was off to obedience school once a week for six months. I would be 'white knuckling' the steering wheel on the drive there and reminding myself quietly to be calm and centred no matter how much 'our boy' wanted to remain a free spirit and do as he pleased. It was always the same. The instructors would demonstrate a new skill for the session, whiz through the steps, and become incredibly upset and condescending to me when I could not pick up the skill ultra fast. I felt like saying, "This is what separates average teachers from decent teachers—the knowledge of how to best improve each individual's learning experience within unique circumstances." Still, it was the weekend, and I was away from the classroom, so I decided not to start this battle.

This has led me to become super self-conscious when I need to explain something to someone other than a student. I must consciously remind myself not to launch into teacher mode when explaining the unknown to non-students. The giveaway of teacher mode is using my teacher's voice. It is firm and decisive and makes anyone you talk to feel like they are back in the classroom. Again, it is not something I set out to do, but there have been numerous times where friends have started to roll their eyes or simply tell me, "Geez, I love it when you condescend to me." They usually follow it up with, "Great work, Teach," or simply flip me the bird. My fiancée is especially a fan.

Duty

You can tell someone is a seasoned teacher by the way they study the duty area maps just before the roster goes live at the beginning of the school year. It is not only the detail in which he/she picks over the map but the fact that they arrived at the table twenty minutes before anyone else. The skill is not to find the perfect place to spend your time, more the necessity of avoiding being stuck somewhere disastrous for the entire year. I once agreed to run history lunchtime tutorials for an entire semester. This was a swap with another teacher so he would take my after-school bus duty for the semester.

What to look for in a decent duty area? Being a tall male, when I first started teaching, I was always placed in the areas where friction may occur. Don't get me wrong; these areas can be exciting, even a little entertaining, but day after day, year after year, they can start to wear on you. A rotation of sites from term to term is what is required here; however, more times than not, this does not occur, and it is the wizard in the administration who has waved their wand, and everything has landed perfectly (at least according to them). This is interesting, as usually all their mates are set up in a nice little area overlooking a single rose bush somewhere.

Equipment needed for duty: For me, the essentials are just a dark pair of sunglasses. The more FBI looking, the better. It is funny: students seem to feel like they can't trust their instincts when they can't see your eyes. I have had multiple occasions where students have walked up to me and ended up confessing something, mistakenly thinking I had been looking at them from across the yard.

These are some of my highs and lows of being on duty:
- In my first year of teaching, I was on lunch duty. Lunch had just ended, and I made my way to my classroom from the other side of the school. I was hurrying students along when the next thing I knew, a student just ran up and cracked a smaller student square in the groin and took off. Little man picked himself up off the ground and was after him, and they disappeared into a classroom down the end of the aisle. When I got in, the little fellow had all

these older lads lined up against the wall belting into them. He was yelling out at everyone while lashing out, "Doesn't matter if it wasn't you! You will get it as well." I had to jump in there to grab him. It was like trying to slow down a manic kangaroo as he bounced along most of the tables in the room.

- In my first ever duty while on prac, I was saddled with a seasoned teacher, someone I had just met for the first time. He pointed towards a few creatures lurking on the outer edges of the oval, crouched behind a makeshift shelter. Smoke rose upwards above them. He told me, "See those students there? You know, and I know they are all smoking, but maybe only make a thing of it if they try to sell you something."
- Fights, fights, and more fights. Lunchtime fights always get the school buzzing. It is like a red-carpet event for the school tough guys. Word has usually gone out earlier that there is going to be a ruckus, then half the school comes out to bear witness.

Mi Casa, Su Casa?

They say humans are creatures of routine and habit. If you ever want to witness a frightening situation, have a graduate teacher take up a seasoned teacher's designated chair in the staffroom. Fireworks are assured.

Maybe it is just teachers' protective nature, or perhaps it is that we are so used to being pushed and pulled in every direction that we need sets of defined parameters to regain some control. For whatever reason, teachers are territorial creatures. These are the typical hot spots around schools where tensions can reach boiling point.

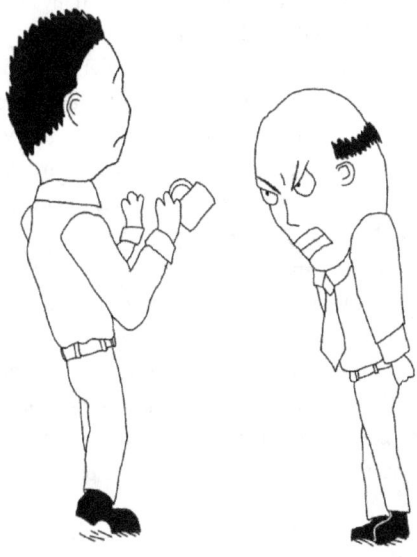

I have witnessed declarations of war issued over the usage of a colleague's coffee mug. It may be convenient, and you may think no one is watching as you reach in the cupboard to pull out the closest mug, but we can sense it, and your day of reckoning will come. The same goes for chairs. It doesn't matter if it is in an office, a conference room, or the outdoor bench for lunch. If you are new to the scene, scan the environment first for dangers before making your move. I still get great pleasure witnessing graduate teachers accidentally sitting in the chair/spot of a twenty-plus year teacher in the staffroom during lunchtime. How you handle this situation is going to tell me a bit about you. When I was a prac student, I had a seasoned teacher (head of the department at the time) tell me very matter-of-factly that I had been sitting in his seat during a morning staff meeting. I hadn't done it on purpose, and there was no particular reason why he had to sit there, but somehow his pride was hurt. I made a mental note to keep the peace and relocate for the next meeting.

This was until later that day when he kept throwing it in my face, so I had to renege on my previous deal with myself. I made a concerted effort to get up early the day of every staff meeting for the remainder of my prac to make sure I was the first one in to take his spot. His face each time he walked through the doors to see my defiance was fascinating. A few years later in my career, I was acting as head of the department for a semester, and I was invited to my first senior leadership meeting. I made sure to get to the meeting extra early and put significant consideration into where my location around the table would be, making sure I didn't sit anywhere I wasn't supposed to. Unfortunately, I ended up in the principal's chair. Later, I found out this information was kept from me on purpose as a 'welcome to the team' prank by the other attending members. The principal didn't even bat an eyelid when he entered the room, sitting at an empty chair while mostly running the meeting on his feet. I only found out later when the rest of the table burst into laughter, finally letting me in on the prank. Guess it comes down to how secure you are in yourself.

Personally-assigned car parks on public school campuses are a rare find. The novelty is usually only designated to the upper echelons of power—

principals, deputies, and the occasional gung-ho registrar. There have been one or two times when a staff member from outside the realm of power has managed to snap up a spot. No one knows how or why this occurred. I once had to endure a staff member at a social event telling me the ins and outs about his reasoning behind why specific staff gets assigned parking spots. It was a backhanded way for him to tell me that he had recently been given a spot, and we should marvel in this greatness, even if he did not choose to use those exact words. I would have let it go, except it went on for forty-five minutes, and there was no let-up to get out of the monologue. Instead, I just made sure to park in his spot for a week straight, arriving extra early and leaving extra late. It is the small things that get me through most days.

Like most situations in life, escalation is a genuine thing. In one school where I worked, the Phys Ed department had 'claimed' the sporting oval next to our classrooms to park their cars. There was no real drama to this at first, except the spots were a super easy walk to the office and nearby classrooms, which also meant you did not have to mess around with the other collective bays on the campus, which seemed to be about a third of the size of any regular parking spot. An office colleague of ours one day took the liberty to park up on the oval but was reminded by several sports teachers throughout the day that this was not acceptable. When hearing the news, we in his office decided to move with solidarity and made a pact to arrive at the same time the following day to take all the spots and continued this for some time. We had considered getting the cleaner to spray paint our names across our new claimed spots, but in hindsight, I think we were just drunk with power by this stage.

End of Year Psychos

By the end of the year, it is not uncommon for teachers to become savages. By this point, teachers are emotionally drained. Students can sense their end-of-year freedom is close, so they kick it up a level with disruptive behaviours—and if you do make it back to your desk alive after class, you have reports, parental contacts, and the following year's planning beckoning your name. Catching the stray eye of a colleague during this time can take on a range of misinterpretations as well as disproportionate responses.

Here are a few suggestions for maintaining a peaceful and productive working environment during these times.

Everyone is busy: Just because you say it the loudest and most often doesn't make you any more important. I have a boatload of respect for my colleague who says nothing yet finishes everything, compared to the old mates who keep voicing how busy they are—actions, not words, good people, and keep an eye on the prize.

Stay professional: When everything starts to pile up, there is an urge to let it out. Unfortunately, this can come at the least expected (and least appropriate) times. I have witnessed professional relationships ruined when a colleague has reached a tipping point and unloads on a staff member nearby. Every morning that I walk through the school gates, I remind myself that I am in a professional space and will conduct myself in this manner. It is not easy and has taken discipline over the years, but there are no blurred lines when I need to interact with colleagues professionally.

Do your best to avoid being petty: Pettiness thrives during these stressful times. Energy levels are low, so it is easy to misinterpret the smallest of details and let them eat at you. My rule of thumb is to give everyone a chance. If a colleague lets me down byways of pettiness, I simply note this and remind myself I do not need to overextend myself when supporting this colleague. The usual response for colleagues is to fight fire with fire, which can be extremely amusing as a bystander. However, nothing is usually achieved except a whole lot of ill will and hurt feelings.

Respect people's personal space and time: If someone is quietly working away, evaluate the situation first before assuming they can't wait to hear your talking point. If you can see your colleague busy at work and are unsure whether now is the right time to lay your monologue on them, maybe start by asking or even just throw out a passing comment, then evaluate the response from there. Nothing irritates me more than someone trying to carry on a conversation with me when I am clearly busy. These days I have a system. I give one polite 'brushoff,' telling my colleague I am sorry I am not trying to be rude, but I need to get this done. Most people are good and understand boundaries. The few who attempt to continue past this point are either arrogant or socially inept, and my response takes on a very different tone while still remaining professional.

Small random acts of kindness: Open a door for someone, notice something good or positive a colleague has done, smile and say hello when you pass a colleague in the hall. All these acts add to a sense of belonging and community that is important within schools.

At the end of the day, you will be spending a significant amount of time around your colleagues, so you may as well make it as productive of a space as possible, even though burning down another colleague's desk can seem like the only viable move at times.

First Impressions

"What do you do for a living?" This question always sends a chill down my spine.

To this day, I do my best to avoid bringing up what I do for a profession when I meet people for the first time, as the responses are always the same. The most common answer is that the person hated maths or was okay with it until the day algebra started showing up. These days, I have trained myself not to respond straight away, a change in my feedback loop which has taken years of discipline. When I was young and naive, I would question these fears. I asked the person what it was in particular about algebra that threw them off. Before I knew it, I would need to spend a large portion of my time reassuring the person that it was not their gaps in knowledge or lacking work ethic that produced these past dismal results. Yes, for sure, your teacher at the time had it in for you, which was totally unacceptable as all you wanted was to be young, wild, and free. The conclusion reached by this person is usually the same. Had it not been for this setback, they would be on the high road in life, achieving miraculous accomplishments and soaring to incredible heights.

The next typical response is from the people who doubt that I am telling the truth. Being a taller gent who enjoys his sports, I can see them working it over in their heads as I speak. Maybe he thinks completing Sudoku once or twice qualifies him to teach maths. A lady actually said to me, just after I had finished introducing myself, "So, you're sure you are not a sports teacher?" As if this was *really* my thing, just rocking up to first meets and lying about the kind of teacher I am.

Sometimes I am seen as competition. People need to measure themselves against others. I remember when I was traveling, I would make my way around the backpacker bars, all the while meeting new people. At one of the bars, they finally managed to get it out of me that I was a maths teacher. I spent the next ninety minutes in a math Olympiad. Every time I went to refill at the bar, another patron deluged me in a barrage of mental maths questions. The loser would buy the drinks. I was in Thailand another time as part of a tour group. There was an elderly couple who were both ex-engineers. As soon as they found out I was in the profession of numbers, every moment was a chance for them to test my knowledge, which, to be honest, had peaked at the three-minute mark into our first conversation on day one. From then on, I spent the remaining weeks just hanging on for the ride.

The final response is from the savages out there who just hate teachers for having holidays. The rage I get from these people is real. I feel like saying, "See all your rage right now? I think there is more to it than just picturing me on holidays every ten weeks." Now, when I meet people for the first time, I just tell them I find x for a living, sometimes I go a little crazy and even go on the hunt for y and z.

Individuals or Cut From a Template?

No one is precisely the same, but in every workplace I have ever worked at, there have been similar characters floating around specific to that industry. These are those characters in the teaching profession.

The young graduate teacher: This character is straight out of university and harnesses a zest for life and all things good in education. They can be a much-needed addition to a department, bringing in their youthful exuberance and passion, but they are known to get a little bit beyond themselves at times and can become overwhelmed. This character will always bring their smile into the office first thing in the morning and usually be the first to put their hands up and take on new tasks. If they have not been spotted for a few hours, check the hallways as they may be sitting in a vacant classroom somewhere fighting back the tears related to the never-ending pile of work and expectations.

The seasoned teacher: This character has a few decades of experience of teaching under their belt, minimum. They have seen at least three to four overhauls of the curriculum and are incredibly sceptical when new ideas are introduced. This character is well aware of themselves, what works and does not work in their mind, and it can take a mountain of effort for them to change their views even slightly. Their professional demeanour can be cold sometimes, and they do not initially play nice with young graduate teachers.

Inspector drama: This character has an incredible skill for sniffing out drama even when it is still in the stages of infancy. The smallest amount of adversity can send this colleague over the top, and before you know it, they have you bailed up in a hallway somewhere, unloading all their frustrations and worries to you even though you didn't ask and now curse yourself for making eye contact when passing. Make sure to measure your responses appropriately when talking with this character, as they can turn any conversation around onto them and produce a monologue of their daily dramas.

Handball Harry: Quickest hands in the west old this mate is. This character will swiftly offload a majority of their weekly tasks on you in the blink of an eye. This character is cunning, and after the initial few times of having you complete tasks for them that you didn't need to do, they realise they now need to approach you differently if you are to pick up any of their work. You should know something is coming when they start a conversation with you with minor praise as they soon will be subtly sliding in whatever tasks they are trying to offload. This character usually has bucketloads of charm and the tidiest desk in the school.

The respected soldier: This character has a deep sense of duty and professionalism, making sure to lead by actions, not words. They have on the coal face (in the classroom) each day, usually taking on the most challenging classes with little more recognition than an occasional thumbs up from a passing principal or the invitation to run a specialised tuition group for students outside of their regular school hours. Their stoic mindset and hardworking nature make these characters highly respected by both staff and students alike. It takes a lot to throw this character off, yet try to mess with their reputation, and you may find a horse's head in the back seat of your car one day.

The difficult one: All of these characters' motives and actions in a teaching environment come from the core belief that they have been misunderstood throughout their careers. Due to this, their protective mechanism is to make every colleague's experience around them a living hell. This character has learned over the years to trust no one and has a checklist of all the current 'beefs' they have with colleagues—complete with ideas and timeframes recorded next to each name for future retribution and 'getting even.'

Mr. 9 to 3: It is actually more like Mr. 8:45 a.m. to 2:55 p.m., but that just doesn't have the same ring to it. This character, in my experience, is more likely to be male and has a knack for executing the start and finish of their working days exactly as the school siren sounds. This character is allergic to taking on any extra responsibility outside of their minimum professional requirements, yet is always the first one to arrive in line at the free sausage sizzle during school activity days, even though he was not involved in the setup procedures.

Sharing is Caring

You learn a lot about people when sharing resources with them: their good character traits, not-so-good attributes, and even the downright mysterious. I believe there should be a level of professional etiquette when sharing, and I think there are ways to handle these situations.

The following list has been my hotspots for drama over the years, along with a few tips to help smooth over those frosty inter-collegial relations.

Sharing classrooms: This is my pet peeve. Every year I put a decent amount of work into presenting my classroom in a worthy educational manner. I am a visual learner, and I believe the more students are surrounded by mathematical concepts, the more likely they are for the learning to sink in, even if it is on a subconscious level. When I walk into my room just after the previous class to find rubbish on the ground, chairs parked around the room, and the teacher desk a mess, I know something must be said. Usually, a quiet word to the teacher is enough. However, when this has been an ongoing situation, I find myself excusing myself as I walk into their lesson to remind students that they are indeed in a classroom, not a barnyard—and to please make sure to erase your masterpieces of work before the next class enters. It is just common decency.

Resources for students: Turning up to class with something to write with is something you would expect most students to achieve; however, it is still a challenge for some staff members. I used to be quite lenient, letting other staff borrow my class set of pencils or erasers, even the calculators. However, my trust was broken a few years back when I was sick and accidentally left my class set of calculators in my classroom. I arrived the next day to find that out of twenty-five calculators, only five remained. I confronted the teacher responsible for the class the previous day and asked if they saw twenty calculators walk out my door. The reply was less than inspiring. To this day, I now keep my supplies up high and out of reach of any passers-by.

Sharing office space: This one is a little tricky and covers a few facets—the first being time constraints. Most teachers, if not all teachers, have huge hearts, and when asked to, they take on more responsibility for no other incentive except for the knowledge that they are a super good person and it may make a difference to students. So, managing your time to complete the plethora of tasks you may stack up becomes essential. It helps to be a good team player and respect others' time. If you see a staff member flat out on a task, don't continue to bug them, but read the cues. On the other side, if you are the one being annoyed, feel free to tell your colleague, "Maybe now's not the best time to tell me about your new kitten and how cute they are…"

This dovetails nicely into office space. Hard borders, that is all I am going to say. I have seen colleagues lose their minds with their personal desk space being invaded. Like anything, communication plays a key role at times of symbolism. I had a bit of a go at piling up many textbooks and labelling them 'the wall.'

Booking the communal computer lab: This area has become the most sought-after commodity in every school I have worked in, and getting any time in there is incredibly rare. Yet, I would always find the same teachers' names booked on the system for a solid term. Now, the booking people will always tell you, teachers can only book a week or two in front, but I believe there is a little corruption afoot, and certain names get looked after. Again, common sense should prevail here. If you have students who need to conduct research or finish assignments, then sure, by all means, book the area. If you are a science teacher and have secured the lab for analysis and most of your students are playing HALO, give up your spot to someone more in need.

Leaving Relief Lessons for Other Staff

Nothing better than heading to my pigeonhole at the start of my day to find an internal relief slip waiting to be handled.

I came across an old relief lesson I had created (one of my first) the other day. It encouraged me to write this. The detail I had put into preparing the lesson was incredible. I am not trying to brag, except to point out that the detail exceeded anything I have ever done since. These days, when I leave relief, if I have three-dot points and the correct room number on my page of notes, I am doing well. There was a time, however, when I pushed for higher standards. These standards can differ significantly in schools. I have picked up relief lessons with paperwork attached that I imagine would make supervisors of Ph.D. students proud. I have also picked up reliefs with barely any information included. For me, if I am taking the relief lesson and have a few instructions outlined to give to students with the correct resources attached, I am good. If you need me to hunt down technology or photocopy your materials for you, I will curse your name.

Here are some of the better relief lessons I have encountered:

'YouTube Sport' was once left for me as a relief assignment from a sports teacher. I laughed to myself when I first looked at the paper and saw the single instruction scrawled across the page. I then asked the relief coordinator where the real relief was, to which he replied, "This is it." It turned out to be the gift that kept on giving. I had a class full of Year Nine terrors, and this was a double lesson that went for eighty minutes. No computers had been booked, and it was before phones were as accessible as they are these days. I did manage to make a last-minute booking in the library for computers but still questioned how educationally sound this lesson would be.

In most schools, the rule of thumb is that for practical subjects like Manual Arts, Music, or Home Economics, if the specialist teacher is away from school, the relief to be left should be theory work. This helps eliminate any issues that may occur with teachers 'not from the specialty area' being in a vulnerable environment. In saying that, I was issued a cooking relief lesson once for a year seven class. For whatever reason, I was left with a practical lesson, and the students were required to cook fried rice. I tried to tell them that we probably should not go through with this lesson, but the looks on their faces were heartbreaking, so we decided to push through. I wish I had not done that. I have never seen so many potential fires break out in such a short period.

Usually, once I know a teacher, they leave me the option for a practical or theoretical lesson if I must cover a lesson for them. I became good friends with a sports teacher at one school. We had ongoing verbal sparring sessions in the weeks previous on which subject was harder to teach, Physical Education or Mathematics. I won't go into the ins and outs of it, but neither of us would give an inch with both of us being proud and competitive beings. However, he gave me a little insight into his world when I picked up his relief one day. I had two options. I could use the box of rubber bananas and condoms that he had delicately laid out for me to teach students about safe sex procedures. Or I could opt for the theoretical approach to introduce the topic using the PowerPoint he had left. Every slide of the PowerPoint just so happened to be a graphic picture of every sexually transmitted disease known to the human race. The nail in my coffin was that students weren't even supposed to be learning about this topic for another three weeks. Well played, my friend.

Photocopy Etiquette

When running smoothly, the photocopier is a blessing. However, when it is not, the real personalities start to show themselves. Ten years of teaching has led me to understand that how you use the photocopier says a lot about you as a person. Below are the common types of photocopier personalities I have experienced this far.

The weak link: The person who is out for themselves. As long as this person has pushed the start button and sees the first paper shoot through the other end, their responsibility is done. They could have two hundred copies to print off, but this person will leave the photocopier, and even if it breaks down, they will find a way to justify how it is not their fault.

Common character traits for the weak link include lack of personal responsibility, immaturity, and being ill-prepared!

I rate this colleague a D grade for photocopier practices. What saves them from an F is my own guilt. Sometimes when this character has a job running through the copier and is not in the office, I see it as my obligation to delete the job. Then, making my way out of the office, it is my sincere hope that by the time my colleague returns, they will understand the link between starting and completing the task and responsibility. This has been a long and tiring lesson so far.

The cursed one: This character always manages to experience the most intense copier jams possible. When you offer to help and look at the flashing items on the console, you feel the intense need to stop for a moment and question how this situation is even possible.

A common character trait for the cursed one is a high level of patience. This is not the person who will attempt to handball the job as soon as the copier jam begins. Instead, this person will persevere, and most of the time will come through and solve the problem. They are also consistent. I don't know whether it is a sign from the universe, but this character always seems to experience the worst jams right before class, and it is usually a class that is going to need a tree's worth of paper just to quiet down in the first five to ten minutes. Countless times I have walked past these characters wrestling with the copier paper drawers first thing in the morning. I can see the plea in their eyes begging, "Please tell me you have seen this type of jam before, and you know the way out!"

I rate this character a B grade. It would be higher, but for the amount of time and effort they direct into their fixing procedures, I feel their process should be more efficient by now.

The tyrant: This character, in their mind at least, is the supreme leader of the copier. They know everything about the copier (whether proven or not) and take it upon themselves to dictate every other staff member's allotted time to photocopy. It is always interesting to note that this character will use the copier the most and typically during peak times.

The tyrant commonly sees their work as the most important and expects this to be remembered by staff at all times. Further, it is never just one or two papers that need copying. Class sets of thirty are standard, and this character will make sure to set up shop at the copier to make sure no one messes with their job. Not one to wait around, as soon as there is even the smallest bit of silence from the copier, the tyrant will jump on the chance to set up shop and begin their eternity's worth of copying.

This character receives a C grade. Although they are pushy and self-absorbed, their mountain of copying usually results in some useful resources being thrown your way. I suspect this is done when a little of their guilt has started to boil over.

The prankster: Fun times at all times is this character's motto. This colleague usually has their desk set in a back corner of the office somewhere with their computer screen tilted so no one can see their copious amount of YouTube playlists piling up on their desktop. This character has an innate ability to sense when other colleagues are heading to the copier. As soon as you are within touching distance of the start button, this colleague will send through a mountain of paperwork, making sure to include their name somewhere on the documents being transmitted through, so you know exactly who is responsible for wasting your time.

I rate this character a C+/B-. Their cheerful and fun nature can be a blessing at times. However, if they want to delve into this role, they need to make sure they are consistent with their effort amongst all colleagues, not just those they are friends with. Fireworks assured.

The professional: There is always talk around schools of this character's existence, yet they are rare. Someone somewhere once saw this character operate. They are professional, and they set the standard for photocopier usage. Their awareness levels are incredible. They have a concise understanding of each colleague's behaviour, knowing precisely the times they should access the copier and, if need be, how to approach each individual if they are desperate for some copying. Although not a machine mechanic, they understand the importance of the need to demonstrate with actions, not words, when in the office, and will make sure they tackle each technical malfunction with grace and even a little gratitude.

This character receives an A+.

The Rat Pack

Rat Pack: *The collective name of several top entertainers who were known to pal around and party*—Urban Dictionary

I was lucky enough to meet my rat pack early on. We were young, wild, and free (mostly) and didn't mind a drink or two after school hours to celebrate the big wins of the day, like students turning up to class on time and not being told to, "Get f##ked," at any point during the day

Here are some of the better stories I can remember.

Front row tickets: Whole school assemblies can be a spectacle. With teachers sitting up on plastic chairs as their class sits on the ground beneath them, your rapport with students and behaviour management skills are on full display. If a student starts acting up and being a nuisance, it is on you to regain control. In my early days, I would leave my perch and sit on the floor next to a misbehaving student. These days, through years of practice, I can shoot a stare in the student's direction long enough for the student to stop. However, with our rat pack being young and competitive beings at the time, it was only natural that we created a level of competition. Setting up members of the pack with a little adversity was not unusual during these times. Pack members were called to the microphone to give impromptu speeches by other pack members or to present certificates to students with all the most problematic names to pronounce highlighted on the list before it was handed over. Members would do their best to rile the class of another member moments before the assembly was to begin. There was even a time or two when a pack member was able to sneak into the front row, knowing another member would be speaking, and make their best attempt to throw the speaker off through low-key wolf whistles and mumbles under the breath. These attempts to break composure and avoid detection from colleagues and the school's administration team were all part of the fun.

This is the cue: During this time, I was a Year Coordinator. I used to get bailed up at all times by staff about the behaviour issues of my cohort. I could be moments away from starting my class, and a staff member from the other side of the school would storm in and demand action in connection with some event that had just happened. I was still early in my career and didn't know how best to handle these situations. I would be stuck in back-and-forth arguments with these staff members, feeling like time was standing still. Over time, members of the pack would develop a system to get me out of these situations, walking over, asking my advice on something, and pulling me away. As time went on, as a unit, we started to develop signals. Unfortunately, we would establish the meanings for most of these different signals when we were on the drink, so it would take some time for the memory of the correct response to kick in. A lot of the time, I just felt like a third base coach throwing any kind of gesture out there, hoping that it would be picked up and understood by *someone*.

The ever insistent: In every school, there is at least one staff member that you can't help but wonder how they are still employed. You may even ask this quietly to another trusted colleague. The usual reply is a gesture towards a filing cabinet with years of subpar performance reports being filed, yet nothing has happened. We had a colleague like this. She was a little mad and knew how to drive staff up the wall, whether she intended to or not. These behaviours intensified when she had nothing to do, so we all made sure to keep her busy. These were a few of the go-to strategies:

Photocopying: The only problem was, it did not matter how detailed you were in both your verbal and written explanation of the task. Your copies would always come back completely different from what you asked for. I had to admire her creativity, at least.

Restock classroom supplies: If we could sense her madness was on the rise and she was becoming a little twitchy, we would ask her to go around and restock classrooms. Staff knew that once she was in a classroom, the potential for all hell to break out was high, so they did their best to keep her from entering. These responses were hilarious if you happened to find yourself in earshot and ranged anywhere from a simple, "No thank you, we are all stocked up," to, "Get the f#ck out now!"

Rearrange and reorder the office fridge: This was not so much a task she was required to do, but more one she enjoyed. The only problem was that she needed to debrief as she was doing it, so any staff members around in the office would be lectured on standards of optimal fridge organisation, product information, and always comparing cross-cultural meal plans.

Leading by example: We all shared the common view amongst the pack that staff meetings were less about the importance of the information being delivered and more about creating fun ways to pass the time. However, our exploits became a little too much, with the school principalship members having to sit at our table to maintain order. A student once saw footage of one of our staff meetings (another teacher was re-watching her presentation, which she had delivered at the meeting, thinking that no student was watching while in class). The student caught up with me and asked, "Sir, you know how you and (other members of the pack) are so big on orderly conduct while we are in your classes? Don't you think it is important that you lead by example?" She laughed as she informed me of the footage she had seen. Oops.

Friday Night

Teaching in the country, school was done by 2:30 p.m. There would always be a crew of teachers in the staff room after, having a drink to unwind. Then from there, people would split up. I always looked forward to the working week's windup, but it was extra special when teaching in the country. We had a group that would try to head out to one of the nearby hilltops on the edge of town. We were lucky that our driver had a four-wheel drive, and he enjoyed the challenge of climbing new heights. A few times, I thought we would be unable to reach the top, but it is impressive what can be achieved with a little perseverance.

We would aim to be at the highest point just as the sun was going down. After school, there's nothing better than a few beers while looking out over a bare landscape with not a whole lot of pointless chatter going on. Once the ritual was complete, we would head back to respective places to shower, reload, and head on out into the night's activities of the town.

I have a feeling the above line might be a little misleading. Sure, there was activity, but not a lot of it—choice of two pubs, one a little superior to the other. We would usually head to the nicer/more modern one, and if you could get there before 6 p.m., you would be in for a happy hour—and usually a Friday night fight with the miners in town who had a few days off, having been on the sauce since early hours. You would get a few hours in, meeting up with various other crews. Your performance for the next hours was a good indicator of whether to shut up shop for the night or head on (usually headfirst by this stage) into the 'Belly of the Beast'

The 'Belly of the Beast' (its reals name escapes me these days) was the local club in town, not a nightclub. My memory is a little hazy, but I am pretty sure it was the local bowling club during the day. Between 8:30 p.m. and 12:00 a.m. on Friday and Saturday, it became alight with laughter and stories from here and there. The fun little added challenge to this premise was that if you were not inside by 10 p.m., you could not get in. They would bring the steel bars down around all the entrances, and the team of muscled-up security would make their presence felt. My favourite part was how supportive my colleagues could be during this time. The few times I rocked up a few minutes late and was summoned to an early night by a security team member, I would see my colleagues on the inside sliding limbs through the bars doing their best to support me with screams of, "You wanker, how hard is it to read your watch and rock up on time?" Another classic was, "Mate, how much do you rate yourself as a maths teacher if you can't even interpret time correctly?"

If you made it in, it was a whole other story. You would be greeted at the bar again by colleagues who had been there for a while and had been putting the work in. Quick Tequila shots x 3 meant you were left alone for an hour or two, whereas the old mate who refused was slammed with various phrases throughout the night, all questioning his worthiness as a human being. The premises shut down at midnight, and the staff had an impressive ability to make sure all patrons were outside by 12:05 am, and the bars were locked down, making sure no one could re-enter. Again, some people saw this as a challenge, and over my time, I did see various kamikaze missions of people trying to re-enter, but it never ended well. This time of the night was the hardest. The skate park opposite was a hangout for the students who would take up various positions in the bushes so you would never see them, but you knew they were there. I don't understand why they were out at this time, but you didn't want to end up being spotted by them. Getting home required a whole heap of planning and navigation. To this day, I still credit these Friday night adventures as the catalyst to developing a robust strategic mindset in the years to come.

Positives and Negatives of Heading Country

Teaching in the country deserves its own chapter to do it any justice, but I will do my best to summarise the best and worst bits.

The Good:

The financial incentives: The further you head away from the city, the more enticing your bonus becomes. Working in the Pilbara, the money came to an extra $10,000 at the time, which for a twenty-five-year-old started an excellent little first deposit into a savings account. Rent was also well subsidised. I think the most I paid in two years was $35 a week.

Career advancement opportunities: I don't think most graduates are necessarily thinking about career advancement prospects straight away, but country service offers a lot more by way of growth opportunities. In my second year, I was asked to take on the role of Year Coordinator, again not a massive part, especially in a small school, but it allowed me to see students outside of the usual class time. There is the flip side to this, with people being promoted into roles they don't necessarily deserve. But this is just part of life.

C-Grade Celebrity Status: If the students liked you and respected you, you almost felt like a C-grade celebrity walking around town. Students would call your name when you were going about your business, sometimes following you in packs wanting to know about your innermost workings. I remember I brought my then-girlfriend up from the city for a weekend. When I arrived back to school on Monday, the students exploded with theories in class. My lady gave me a call when she returned to the city a few days later. She had been seated on the plane next to one of my students, who was heading down for a few weeks. She reckons it was a solid 90-minute drilling of what Sir was like out of school.

Adventures: Being surrounded by nothing but bush in either direction can either make you or break you. For me, I loved it. Heading out of town in an off-road capable vehicle provided endless adventures and memories of hitting those secret spots which most people didn't know to see. Some of the sunsets I caught from a hilltop were incredible. Some of the mechanical breakdowns I experienced in the middle of nowhere were heartbreaking at the time, but I look back on them as character-building moments.

The Not-So-Good:

Student Revenge: Living in a town where everyone knows everybody else, it is hard to escape some of the unpleasant times in class. I am not saying that you should avoid disagreeing with students out of fear of retribution, but as with all things in teaching, walking a fine line is the key. There were incidents in my time where students had vandalised teachers' cars and other personal property. A few students even broke into a female teacher's house one time while she was not home, shattering most of the windows and leaving a note on the kitchen table spelling out precisely what they had disliked about her and her lessons over the previous week.

Housing: If you were a teacher and had been in town for a bit, you were usually set up in one of the bigger and nicer houses in town. If you were young, single, and new—like I was when I first started—you had to put up with a shack on the edge of town. When I arrived for the first time, I remember staring out my living room window, seeing nothing but dirt. The teachers' housing council was made up of representatives from the high school and the primary schools in town. Overhearing some of their conversations, at times, you could swear that they thought they were the most significant powerbrokers in the free world. It was just unfortunate that their efficiency didn't always match their delusions of grandeur.

Repairs around the house could also become a point of contention. Due to specific insurance policies, repairs were only to be handled by the government agency. This was all good and well if they were in town when the fixing was required. If not, this soon became a nightmare. I knew a teacher who waited three years to have his oven repaired. This was while he was making fortnightly phone calls to the agency to check up.

Boredom: It doesn't matter how long you have been in town. Eventually, boredom will kick in. Usually, you could ride it out, picking up a new hobby for a while. I once went through my kitchen drawers for a few days and re-sharpened all my kitchen knives. Other people would drink themselves unconscious. One colleague had a Sunday morning ritual of driving 180km to a particular service station just to purchase a can of coke. He told me he found it meditative.

Drama, Drama, Drama: There was a pattern of behaviour here amongst the teaching circle. I would see new young teachers arrive who would insulate themselves with only fellow teachers, failing to break out and meet new people in the town. Initially, they were all friends, using phrases such as, "I can't believe we are already besties," and, "I think our meeting was meant to be." This was common in the first few weeks. However, come mid-way through term two (or the dog days as I came to know them), these relationships would soon break down with all types of drama kicking off. If you were lucky enough to be staying in the block of flats for single teachers, you would see all kinds of reactionary behaviour, including all-out cussing matches across the courtyards to punch-ups in the car park. One new teacher took one fallout so badly, they locked themselves in their apartment for three days and nights, refusing to leave or have anyone in.

Finally, like everything in life, what you put in is what you get out. I went into my country experience with an open mind and reasonable expectations. I left with some of my fondest memories in life and a wealth of valued friendships.

Practical Experience Number One

My first round of teaching practical experience was at a low socio-economic school, one of the lowest in Perth. I started teaching because I wanted to make a difference, so there was no better place to start.

The days leading up were a rollercoaster of emotions. At times I was nervous. Other times I was overconfident. I knew, being twenty-two years old, I couldn't yet be a good role model for future generations. Fake it till you make it was the phrase that kept running through my mind. For the four-week prac, I observed and taught mainly Society and Environment classes with a Mathematics class here and there. My mentor was a male Art teacher. Due to low student numbers enrolled in the art program, he found himself with an abundance of spare time, which led to him mentoring me. He meant well. He had a good heart. I just don't know how invested he was in teaching.

Each day he would make the same announcement to me. "I like your lesson plan. Do you mind if I make a copy to add to my file?"

"Not at all," I would reply.

At first, I was excited that a seasoned teacher wanted to make copies of my lesson plan. Down the track, I found out that he taught the same course in Society and Environment next year due to student numbers in art dwindling, so he was getting an early jump on his preparation. Soon after, he talked me through his process of making the perfect sandwich, taking great delight in explaining the details. "The secret is using three pieces of bread as well as doubling down on the slices of meat," he would profess to me. He also had a special talent. He always found himself needing to go to the toilet ten minutes into the lesson. He would reassure me he would only be five minutes, then miraculously return with only a few minutes left in the lesson.

Two weeks passed, and my assessor came out to view one of my lessons. I have never prepared one as thoroughly since. The lesson went well. As a class, we had an excellent rapport, and I had made sure we had gone through all the relevant questions in the days leading up to the lesson. The assessor was a little confused when several correct answers were delivered to me before I had finished the question, but hey, at this stage of the teaching game, I was going to take any little point of leverage I could get to keep my head above water.

Duty could be exciting. Talking to different staff members about experiences they had made the time fly. One teacher told me that individual sections of the school had been unattended for years due to several teachers being hit by bricks out of the bushes over consecutive weeks. Others had stories from students' fights in which they had tried to intervene only to be struck at one point. One elderly teacher told me he had made a special point to lock his bicycle up in front of his classroom each day to avoid any harm coming to it, only to see it ridden past him a few days later by a student he had sent out of his class a few days earlier for a behaviour issue.

Practical Experience Number Two

While completing my Diploma of Education, our University Curriculum Coordinator mentioned that certain rural schools were offering incentives to attract teachers. There were only a few schools on the list, and although the financial incentives would be small, it beat taking verbal abuse from drunk customers at the bar I was working at during this time. An adventure to the far Northwest of the state began.

My friend and I signed up and then didn't think too much about it as the date to fly out was still months away. The week before taking off, I decided to search online to see where our school was located. Initially, I thought it was situated on the coast, so in the worst-case scenario, if I had a tough day at school, I could just head out to the ocean to unwind at the end of the day. You could imagine my bemusement when I could find nothing at the supposed location of the school. It wasn't until I went 400km inland and zoomed-in over a patch of red dirt that I finally found it. Glad I put the required amount of research into that one. The flight out followed the same amount of lacklustre preparation, with my friend and I both having decent (separate) nights out and only just arriving in time to catch our flight.

When we landed, the first thing that struck me was the heat. It was only early September, but it was hot. Being driven around town, we were introduced to the various landmarks. Big Hill, East Town, West Town, Road out of town, and place of work (the high school). A perk was that the house we would be sharing was situated directly across from the school. I couldn't help myself from pointing out that at least the morning bus trip wouldn't take too long. I didn't receive the fits of laughter I was expecting.

My Major area for teaching was Society and Environment, with a minor in Mathematics. Initially, I was to take the top year ten class for maths, but with a chasm of self-doubt opening up inside me, I managed to negotiate a switch to the bottom year nine class. To this day, I am not sure such a move has ever been replicated. What a class this would be!

Other memorable events that occurred during my Practical Experience were:

Potato adventures: The first time we went food shopping, I bought a 5kg bag of potatoes. I made sure to grab some steak as well, as I felt a little odd just carrying around a sack of potatoes. My parents are Irish, so we were brought up on the potato's magic and all its wonder. After ten days straight living on boiled potatoes, my mate started to feel sorry for me. He suggested that maybe I should try frying the potato instead of boiling it. This tip elevated me to a whole new realm of happiness.

Template troubles: I created an answer template for my year Eight Society and Environment assignment. I had written everything out a few nights previously, then by mistake, shuffled my template in with my students' assignments. I managed to create a new answer template, this time typing it out, although I did have moments of DeJa'Vu when doing this. I recovered this document again when I began marking students' work. I swore to myself for a good three to four minutes about the atrocity of the letter formation and use of grammar by this particular student, only to soon realise that, indeed, it was my own previous solutions template.

Buddy rooming records: I set a brand-new record for buddy rooming students. It was not my intention to be chasing records straight out of the gate, but if you had seen this year nine class, you would not have been surprised.

Can You Tell Straight Away?

I was asked once by a non-teaching mate if I could immediately tell if someone would make a good teacher when they first started. I had to pause for a moment. I had never applied a lot of thought to it before. I soon became annoyed at myself as I felt that it was something I definitely should have considered.

When I think about it these days, it is like anything. The more you do something, the better you will become at it, at least in theory. However, I believe there can be telling signs early on that someone may struggle in the teaching profession. The following is a list of red flags I have experienced when working with pre-service teachers over the years.

You must want to do it: If you are just in teaching for the holidays, this will unravel you. I have seen too many jaded teachers turn up to work every day to just go through the motions of constant grind and battles. Be happy that you get to help people each day. This will have its trials and tribulations, no doubt. But life is too short. If you are not in it for the right reasons, start looking elsewhere.

Be prepared and organised: Most student teachers excel at this. However, I have had pre-service teachers rock up to me five minutes before a lesson telling me that, unfortunately, they were not able to get their planning done as they hit a hot streak in their card game last night. I bit down on my frustration. "No worries,' I replied. "I guess it is time to introduce you to the five-step lesson plan." I made sure to count each step from five down to one as we made our way into the classroom. "Good luck," I announced as we walked in for sixty minutes of Year Eight Mathematics.

Don't threaten students: You would think this would be super-obvious. I have never witnessed this personally. I have heard stories about student teachers, the day before they were to be assessed, threatening their students to be on their best behaviour. One teacher even told me they had to cease a prac student's time at their school after multiple students had reported that the prac teacher was telling students under his breath, "If you do not behave, there is going to be a lot of repercussions," while the assessment of his lesson was underway. I do think he may have used different, less professional wording.

Be a professional: Don't aim to be the student's best friend. Be firm but fair and set boundaries for the students. One of the most significant learning curves in the early years is to realise that respect needs to be earned both from teacher and student. You should avoid walking into the classroom and expecting blind respect.

Emotional balance and patience: This was a tough one for me when I first started. When a lesson starts heading south quickly, I would feel myself physically choking back the rising anger. The constant conscious effort to remain calm and patient took years of honing. I tell teachers when they first start, it will help you in the long run if you can stay centred and calm.

Like Father, Like Son

One year, I was asked to help out with the school enrolment team. My first session turned out to be something for the ages.

A family from the Middle East came walking through the door. There were three family members in attendance: father, older brother (whom I had taught previously), and younger brother I was to enrol. After initial introductions and niceties, I asked the younger brother what he hoped to do once he finished school. Before he could open his mouth, his father instantly shot back, "Medicine."

"Righto," I told myself. I better get some indicators on ability here before I sign someone up to work in a career that is responsible for life and death. After twenty minutes and more timeless conversation with the father, the younger brother returned with his tests. I marked up and then announced that a combined mark of three out of forty for both the English and maths tests had been achieved. "Not to worry," I told him. "This does not mean your dreams of serving in the medical industry are over for good, but we will need to take a different tack for now." Again instantly, the father spoke up and announced that his son would like to pursue teaching. I had a feeling that this wasn't younger brother's burning desire either, but when I asked him if this is what he wanted, he gave me half a shrug, so onward we went.

There was only one unit left to choose before we would be complete. There was no other day except Friday available for this particular course. It turned out that the younger brother didn't do school on Fridays, so now teaching was off the table as well. I screwed up my work and threw it into the bin, doing my best to bite down on my frustration. After a quick family meeting to the side, it was decided that the younger brother would pursue a mechanics trade. I made sure to ask multiple times, was this what he wanted to do before I took any action of picking up my pen again. The third time through went smoothly, although his father did stop me at one point and mentioned that he would like to head back to school and pursue a career in politics. I told him I would have to enrol him another time. He didn't laugh.

The most bizarre part of this whole experience happened after we had finally completed the enrolment process. Father asked if I would pose for photos with him and his sons. Before I could even reply, he just turned to my colleague, who was sitting next to us, threw his phone at him, and said, "Take a picture." There were snaps of handshakes, numerous position rotations, all combined with individual and group photos. When we finally completed our photoshoot, we said our goodbyes, and they left. I turned to my colleague and asked him if that was the norm. "No. Definitely not," was his reply.

Maths is Not My Specialty

When I completed my degree in Economics, I had no idea what I wanted to do. However, it was clear that I didn't want to spend my life chasing money around, so I was glad that I had dedicated the previous four years at university to honing this skill. When I was in high school, my mother always told me that I should be a teacher, to which I replied, "I don't think so," in a different and nowhere near calm or composed way.

I finished up my Diploma in Education, then headed to the country for my practical experience. In the final week of prac, I was offered a position to stay on at the school, but it was to be in Mathematics, not in Society Environment, which was my major. Not to worry, how hard could this be? I thought to myself. Very f''cking hard would be the answer, as I would soon find out.

Here are a few obstacles I found hard to overcome in my career teaching Mathematics:

Not being confident enough in my content knowledge: Fake it till you make it is a saying that I have become very familiar with, as mentioned. This was particularly profound in my earlier days when I was more concerned about speaking in front of a group of people than having my mathematical knowledge up to scratch. Luckily enough, most of the schools I worked at within my first five years were all challenging, so being strong in behaviour management strategies took precedence over being a master of the curriculum, which tended to favour me. If I looked over the work the night before, this was usually sufficient preparation for the lesson the following day—and if I didn't, hey, no worries, I would fake it till I made it. This coupled well with my strong sense of pride. If I were to make a mistake on the whiteboard during a lesson and the students were to pull me up, I would back myself to the hillside whether I was right or wrong. Now, if something was blatantly incorrect, then there was no denying it. Still, if I could sense hesitation in a student's questioning, I would throw out all kinds of terminology and logic to persuade the student into accepting my answer. "Sir, but the answer at the back of the book is different from yours," was a phrase that could be heard rippling through my classroom walls earlier in my career. I would then have to explain that a math textbook can have errors (usually not many) and a lot less than I intended.

However, this all changed when I started teaching more technical and specialised content to upper school students. Generally, they were very strong with their fundamentals. I remember my first year teaching this course. I thought I would stick to the same game plan and ride it out without having to put in much work. The students were very nice about it; instead of saying, "Sir, this is becoming a little bit ridiculous with the majority of your answers differing from the answers in the text," they just calmly reassured me that they thought my logic had gone askew somewhere and they would stick to their findings, which matched up to the textbook. Thank God they did. At the end of the first term, I pulled the pin to teach this course, swapping with another teacher. I felt too ashamed of my lack of knowledge to continue.

Several years later, I ended up teaching the course again at a different high school. I vowed to myself at the start of the year that I would do everything in my power to learn the ins and outs of the curriculum, which usually meant spending two to three hours a night for that year researching the content, preparing my slides, and answering the questions from the exercises. I have now been teaching the course for a few years, and my confidence has grown in leaps and bounds; however, I still have times where my self-doubt sneaks up on me to do me in. Fortunately, the textbook and I are generally in agreement on the answers these days.

Teaching relevance: "Okay, so there are the steps, now do these 120 questions for the remainder of the period." This is how I was taught maths, and this is how I tried to teach maths in my initial years.

"Sir, what do we do when we finish these questions?"

"Pages 112-115," or whatever the next relevant section was, would be my usual answer. No wonder my less passionate students became even more unenthused.

I don't want to say it was hard to make maths sexy as that just sounds weird, but if students had the choice between crunching numbers for a period or doing a critical writing task on a movie they had just watched, I imagine most of the students would pick the latter. Nothing better than having to teach trigonometry to a bunch of year nine students during the last period of the day. You should see them roll their eyes as we head on out to measure the height of the school's flagpole and the length of the shadow it casts for the fifth time that week. My favourite is when we start to work on algebraic concepts. I begin to introduce X and Y, and within minutes I will have the standard, "When will we ever use this, Sir?" I had a colleague once who became so sick of hearing this particular response that he would simply reply to the student, "For you, probably never."

Writing on the whiteboard: I imagine this sounds like a meaningless task to a lot of you. You probably have perfect cursive writing, and your letter formation is impeccable. I envy you. I genuinely do. I must print all my letters in capitals, and usually, that is not even enough as I hear students quietly questioning their neighbour with, "Is that the letter z or the number 2?" during note-taking sessions. These days, I have fun with it and tell the students, "Okay, team, here are your notes. You have ten minutes to copy down what you think it says. Then, I will come back and read it through." Students have a great time, but it just reinforces that there may have been something to having me last in my primary school class for using a pen.

Bursting Hopes and Dreams

"I want to be a doctor, Sir."
"Nice. You are currently sitting on 13% for the year."

Towards the end of the year, Year Ten students will undergo course counselling with a mentor/selected teacher to help with their upper school courses selection. On paper, my position as a course counsellor means that I provide a pathway for students to link their endeavours for post-schooling to their subjects choices in years eleven and twelve. However, most of the time, it feels like I am bursting the students' hopes and dreams and leaving them devastated.

The opening sentence is not an unusual conversation I have with students. They see the nobility in studying a course like medicine to help people along with the sense of pride they would have from gaining acceptance into such a course. Unfortunately, most of the time, academic achievement, work ethic, and perseverance don't align with the student's hopes and dreams. Here my position becomes a little tricky. I remind the student that nothing is impossible if you are willing to work at it. Still, while we are here, we should remember those strings of assessments at the beginning of the year that sent you into meltdown, so we may need to improve our handling of pressured situations. Your sporadic attendance throughout the year will also need serious improvement.

Trending careers is a thing as well. The number of students who have proclaimed to me over the years that they were going to head into commercial law and make millions seems to correlate closely and coincide well with whatever new commercial law TV show was currently making the rounds at that time. Again, I remind the students, "It is great that you have this ambition, but see here where you have a D grade on your report card next to English, along with a comment from the teacher that explicitly states, "Student X hates to read?" Do you feel that this may be a limiting factor to your success in this field?

For Mathematics, we use diagnostic tests. It is a list of questions that are considered core skills for the unit to be undertaken. There is a set score the student needs to achieve to be deemed a chance of success in the course. However, as the years have progressed, there seems to be a widening gap between students who want to do the course and their actual aptitude. These days, it looks as if you just rock up to your interview and tell the counsellor you will work hard. Whether you intend to or not, this will usually have you placed in the course anyway. Again, this becomes a headache for the teacher having to take the class the following year, as the pace required to deliver all the content in time requires a certain ability level. Spending copious amounts of time in a debate with the student after class hours is not uncommon in these situations.

I had a student recently who fits this mould. He was a mid-year enrolment, and after sitting the diagnostic test and recording a score of 3 out of 20, I recommended to him that the pace and technicality of the mathematics course he wanted to head into would be too much. He assured me he was up to the task.

Here are some of the highlights for this student (Student X) in my mathematics class for the remainder of that year:

Technology challenges: Student X and calculators were not friends. Six weeks into the course, Student X appeared at my desk and asked me, "Sir, how do I turn the calculator off?"

I looked at him quizzically, then gestured towards the button with off written above it. I then asked, "What have you been doing for the last six weeks to turn it off?"

He replied, "I just let the batteries run out then replaced them." Another time he had left his calculator at home and had to borrow one of mine. Again, he asked, "Sir, how do I turn this calculator off?"

Again, I replied, "Still the button that has off written above it."

Assessments: Assessments became the most self-defeating sticking point. Student X managed to score two lots of zero percent on two different assessment items, having answered every question and being the last student to leave the room each time.

Apparel: My highlight is, one particular day, I had entered the Mathematics Office to retrieve some resources for the class I was currently teaching. Student X was also in the office seeking the assistance of any male staff member who would help him with his pants belt buckle, which he had fastened too tight and could not undo.

> I'm going to do medicine.
> Also I can't undo my belt by myself.
> I did it up too tight.

Growing Pains

People hate Mathematics. I know this as people offer this up to me regularly, even though I never ask. However, reminding myself not to turn completely savage, I try to steer the interaction towards being a self-reflective tool for the hater. I let them hear their own words and hopefully come to their own solutions to overcome adversity. Unfortunately, most of the time, it just turns into an aggressive monologue, which has taken the tone of, "I hate everything maths, hear me roar."

These are the common areas I have experienced that lead to the most angst for current and ex-students alike when working with Mathematics:

Relevance: "When the f*ck will we ever use this?" is a familiar catchcry from students that can be heard daily as they slam their textbooks shut and launch their pens across the room in frustration. Initially, I thought if I could just 'pretty up' the lesson and throw in some manipulatives, games, or web activities, students would be so bedazzled by my showmanship they would not realise I had no idea what I was doing. Improving my knowledge of mathematics over the years and linking concepts and skills to their relevance in everyday life have had a profound impact on my lessons.

Boredom: It is hard to get excited about pages in a textbook day after day. "Here are 100 questions to attempt, better get on with it," or, "Sir, what is today's work?" "Pages 115-121" are lesson plans that should not get a look in anymore.

Not wanting to struggle: *"Thinking is the hardest work there is, which is probably why so few engage in it,"* was said by Henry Ford. Most students don't want to struggle. I know I did not when I was at school. People would say to me, "But that feeling you get once you finally figure it out is what I do it for." I would just shrug my shoulders and remind myself that maybe greatness is not for everyone. A go-to line I have in class when I can sense the struggle is becoming real is to remind students that some of the best mathematicians in history weren't necessarily born gifted. They just learned to enjoy the struggle. The usual response is, "Sir, is a mathematician like a magical maths person?"

Fear of failure: We all fear failure. It sucks, but we learn to handle it better and see it for its worth as we mature. Students must go through it in adolescence, a time when self-worth and esteem are hanging on a knife's edge. We need to have students understand that failure does not define them, and if they learn from it, it no longer needs to be their sworn enemy. Worst case scenario, those right-angled triangle problems will become a little less daunting.

Assessments

"This assessment will determine your future career and, for most of you, the kind of life you will have. I hope you are ready."

I hated assessments when I was at school. Generally, I hated school, but assessments frustrated me. I would be able to do the work most of the time, but if someone put an allocation of marks next to a question, a specific time frame, and the stamp of 'official assessment' on the paper, within fifteen minutes, I would be conjuring up all kinds of not so fun thoughts.

The above (opening sentence) is something I say to my upper school students during their initial assessments at the beginning of the year. I make sure to do it with a straight face and let the tension and trepidation build in the room for a few minutes before I break into a smile, easing the student's minds with, "This is just one assessment at one point in time, and many of the world's greatest people have had plenty of failures to overcome." This usually puts the majority of the class at ease. However, there is that one student who is already too far gone who is silently headbutting their table.

I usually guide my students through a complete revision five-ten minutes before their assessment is to begin. No real value-adding can be done here; it is more just to get their mind into gear and focus on the task at hand. I tell them that they are free to get together in groups and work with each other, but I will not be assisting them during this time. Over the years, I learned the hard way that trying to cover two to three weeks of content in three minutes with multiple students is not feasible.

As a courtesy, just before we are to begin an assessment, I mention some things. Timing of the assessment, if the assessment has different parts to it, where to write your name, and I always make sure to sign off in the same way: "Now, once the assessment starts, I can only reread the question to you and nothing more." I hope that students understand that I cannot answer the question for them no matter how creatively they think they can manipulate the sentence, "Sir, just checking if my approach here is the right way to answer this question?"

Students will quickly become ambassadors for the 'mistreated or unjust.' They write annotated notes next to the question as to why they feel they should be exempt. Most of their arguments centre around having forgotten to revise for this part or remembering how to do it, just not right at this instance, and I should consider this when marking.

The final weeks for a year twelve student are full of mixed emotions. Students have put the work in. Now they are starting to see the light at the end of the tunnel. However, there is a smaller group of students who find that reality has now just dawned on them. Over the years, I have had numerous students come to me during these weeks to tell me, "Sir, I am going to do good now and start to do the work; what will I need to do to pass?" I want to say, "Nice one; all you need to do is average 115% across your final three assessments." Instead, I congratulate them on their newfound work ethic and reassure them that I look forward to their improvements.

Online Learning During a Pandemic

The world was thrown into chaos. We knew the virus was on its way over to us, but we didn't know how long it would take to get here. We did know that once it arrived, it would spread like wildfire.

Corona hitting the teaching world was crazy. A week or so after the virus first hit, we were told schools would be shutting down, so we had to figure out a way to deliver lessons online for term two. This became particularly tough for schools like ours where students don't have a heap of money, digital devices, or internet access, which some people consider must-haves heading into the world of online learning. That and the average age of our teaching staff was 55, with most staff having spent the last decade and a half trying to outrun the use of technology within the classroom. Conversations between staff during this time were the best. Everyone was trying hard to reassure each other that they were fine, showing no weakness while anxiety was peaking through the roof. It was like listening to podcasts at 1.5 speed. I have never seen so many eyes so wide open before.

For the last week of term, students were kept at home as teachers scurried around using the time to develop and deliver online learning programs. For my more self-motivated students, this type of learning was great. They were able to log in, and through video conferencing tools, I could deliver my lessons to their screens, all from the comfort of their own home.

Students lacking self-motivation found this style of learning challenging. It was a win if I had five students logged in by the end of the session. Three could figure out how to turn their screen on; this was another little win out of those five students. From little things, big things grow, I guess.

By the first week of term two, teachers and most students were back in classrooms. Further online learning seemed to cease at this point.

These are my main takeaways from my online experience.

- My teaching became way more effective, being able to lock students outside of my digital classroom compared to them just physically breaking the door down and walking back into class.
- I still don't understand how every teenager has a phone and is on their phone all day, yet, getting them to sign up to an online platform using their student email crashes their minds.
- Just because I say I am monitoring your assessment even with my screen turned off may or may not mean I am doing house chores.
- Even with a digital whiteboard, everyone still wants to draw the biggest dick on it.

www.ingramcontent.com/pod-product-compliance
Lightning Source LLC
Chambersburg PA
CBHW070308010526
44107CB00056B/2531